Healing from Heaven

For Terry,
With many blessings
Judith Sakle

Healing from Heaven

Judith S. Sable

iUniverse, Inc.

New York Lincoln Shanghai

Healing from Heaven

iUniverse, Inc.

For information address:
iUniverse, Inc.
2021 Pine Lake Road, Suite 100
Lincoln, NE 68512
www.iuniverse.com

ISBN: 0-595-31493-7

Printed in the United States of America

Contents

Preface

I have never been struck by lightening. I have never had a near-death experience. I am not crazy. I am just like you. I am your average middle class American—but like many, I have conversations with God and angels. Did you know that God makes house calls? This book on healing is a direct result of my divine communications. (My part of our conversations can be found in the words that are written in Italics.)

My divine conversations did not begin until later in life. When I was a child any inclination I may have had towards metaphysics was effectively squelched by pragmatic parents. I always knew that there must be more to life, but I put that idea to rest on a shelf. I proceeded through life doing what was expected of me by my parents. I graduated from Case Western Reserve University in Cleveland, Ohio and got married. I began teaching at a local high school in 1969 and earned a master's degree from Trinity College in Hartford, Connecticut. After five years of marriage, we had our first child. Our second child came three years later. I was emulating my mother by raising a family, tutoring, being a Girl Scout leader, and actively participating in and holding offices in women's organizations.

My life began to change when I decided to switch teaching fields. I joined a cosmetic company and began to teach skin care and glamour techniques. It was at this time that my interest and skills in healing became evident. I believe in the old adage "when the student is ready the teacher appears." I had a client call me one day to ask if I would give a facial to her elderly friend that was just coming out of the hospital. I was happy to comply. While we were talking during the facial I learned that she had been a medium for sixty-seven years. Thereafter, I would visit her every month or two. We would sit in her kitchen and visit with other mediums. They answered many of the questions that I pulled off of my childhood shelf. They recommended books and I began to read voraciously. I joined a local psychic development circle and participated for seven years.

It was during those seven years that I began to attend numerous courses and lectures on metaphysics and healing. I became registered as a medium and spiritual counselor through the Arthur Ford Academy of Mediumship in conjunction with Delphi University in Georgia. It was also during this time that I began my conversations with God.

I strongly believe in reincarnation. I knew that I had to release some old baggage that was impacting this life from a past life. What was revealed as part of this releasing process was that I was angry with God. I found myself actually screaming at God and crying hysterically. When I had completed my tirade, I clearly heard a voice say to me, "Now you can be at peace." I went from complete hysteria to total peace within thirty seconds. I just knew from the miraculous way that I felt that I was speaking with God. We have been having conversations ever since that time.

I started my own development and meditation group in 1994 and have been teaching metaphysics in my town's Adult Education program and in New York City. In 1998 I became certified and registered as a hypnotherapist and have been adding Neuro-Linguistic Programming to my credentials.

My thanks and gratitude goes out to my wonderful family who has been so supportive and encouraging. I would also like to thank the lovely ladies of my book club who graciously contributed their editorial input.

I wish for each individual reading these pages to know the hope, the relief, and the joy that I have felt in sharing them.

Judith S. Sable

PART I
Healing Your Attitude

1

Thoughts from Heaven

The following information is a direct result of my conversations with God. I have presented it to you just as it was given to me. Rather than put most of the book in quotation marks, I have put my part of the conversations in italics. These are the words that were said to me:

My intention in delivering this book is to bring to the general public information that is written in easily understandable concise words. Judith, I know that you wish for this book to be somewhat different than those already in the bookstores and that your main concern is that people learn how to make life changes and to heal themselves. Healing from Heaven will bring this message to the understanding of all: it is you, on some level, who create all within the framework of your lives and it is within your power to heal and to change. It is simple, really, and it begins with a change in thinking.

My angelic messengers will also contribute to the writing of this book. In these pages, we will show you why you have created the diseases within yourselves and give you ways to remedy them. I know that many will call blasphemy a book that is written by God and my heavenly emissaries. I hope that by now, I have sent enough other material so that this therapeutic book will be more widely accepted. This book not only faces philosophical doubters, but also defies some of mainstream medicine. Scientists will probably continue to try to analyze every phenomenon that appears to be unexplainable. There have been enough documented so-called "miraculous healings" that the way has been paved for the truth. Yes, there have been many books written that deal with healing oneself. I send to you this additional book as my gift because of the importance of the information contained within its pages.

I know that many of you will say that you have read many books and that you are saying affirmations, meditating, and visualizing, but you are still not healthy. I say to you, and I have put it in its own chapter, that the key to healing is having belief and absolute faith that you do have control over your own being. You have read that I fashioned you in my image. In truth that is so. I do not speak of physical image. I speak of energetic image. I speak of capabilities. I speak of qualities. Each creation has some of my qualities but my main wish for each of you is that you learn to be who you are. I imbued each of you with creativity and talent. Now it is your choice of how to use that.

There is a saying that for everything there is a purpose unto heaven. That is so. There are neither accidents nor coincidences. You are the creators of what happens to you. Before you decided to incarnate you chose that which you wished to experience. (Some of you wish to think of these experiences as "lessons.") Your soul knows your agenda and sees to it that you have the opportunities to experience your choices. Your soul will not override your conscious mind.

You have the free will of choice and by these choices you enable yourself to have every kind of experience.

God, may I please interrupt here for a moment?

Of course.

You have just said that the soul will not override the mind. In this book you discuss diseases like cancer. No one would consciously choose such a disease and you said that the soul helped to create it for that person's experience.

All right, I see that I will have to elaborate. There is no dis-ease that cannot be healed by anyone—if that is what he truly desires on a soul level. People say they would like good health but try to remember that they created for very good reasons whatever the condition is to be experienced. I know what you are thinking, "Who would not wish to heal themselves of cancer or some debilitating disease?" Yes, on a conscious level that is probably true. Remember, however, that it is the spirit or soul that creates the opportunities.

You made a blueprint of sorts as to what you wished to experience before you elected to incarnate. In that plan you expressed a desire to realize things like tolerance, being non-judgmental, generosity, inner strength, and independence. You did not anticipate every little detail as to every step of your existence or every second of every day. The chart was one of a general nature. Some circumstances were pre-planned, but the soul may choose how to have an experience at any time during one's lifetime.

Then it was necessary for you to erase your memories before you began your life so that you could fully experience your desires. Your conscious mind began this life with a fairly blank slate. Your soul, however, knows everything and will do whatever it takes to help you to remember who you really are. You are a part of me. You already know everything that you need to know and you have but to remember. That is what you are here to do. Your soul, therefore, leads you into the situations that will help you to remember and to give you to the opportunity to learn your desired lessons. If it is for your highest good to have cancer or any other disease then that is what may happen. It is your soul that decides if having a disease would best afford you the experience desired. Yes, you choose on a soul level to get cancer or aids or the flu. The soul may choose, however, to have the experience in ways other than creating disease. Where the conscious mind exerts free will is in your attitude. How will you react to the circumstances set forth by your soul? How will you react to the circumstances that you draw to yourself?

I am still stuck on the soul not over-riding the mind. You said that the key is belief and absolute faith. Are you saying that if the mind continually repeats to itself that it will never get cancer, for example, and comes to completely believe and <u>know</u> that it will never get cancer, the soul will have to find another way to "learn its lesson?"

Yes, that is correct. The soul has many ways from which to select to have an experience. The mind, however, is very powerful and is a partner in creation.

Are you're saying that if I get the flu it's not just because I'm tired, my resistance is lowered, and I'm around people who are sneezing and coughing?

No. Before you came, you may have said, "I wish to experience the flu because it will show me that I need to establish communication between my body and my mind. It will teach me to honor having a body." At some time, therefore, during this lifetime, you will get the flu. If this was not in your plan or if your soul feels that it would not serve you, you would never get the flu this lifetime.

If we got the flu once and experienced it, why would we get it again?

You may repeat it because, perhaps, subconsciously it created the situation where by you could experience other things.

We could experience things like getting more attention.

Yes.

Why would someone choose cancer, aids, or any painful or debilitating disease?

Because sometimes the experience is not just for that person but as a gift of love so that another can have a particular experience. Many times people make contracts with another as part of their pre-planned agenda.

If someone has cancer, others can't experience their pain or treatments.

No. Usually if someone's soul chooses a disease like cancer, it's for a personal experience, but not always.

What lesson would anyone want that would cause his soul to choose such a disease?

Cancer patients can know trust, love, self-love, personal strength and determination, or faith. They can also cause someone else to awaken to loving, caring, or community awareness.

Internalizing rage can bring about some of these diseases but not all people who are angry get sick.

No, it is only if they chose to have that particular experience. The soul would then find a way to bring on the condition. Accumulated anger or stress is one way to induce conditions like ulcers, cancer, polyps, or digestive disorders that "eat you up" internally.

Why would a soul choose something that would be so painful either physically or emotionally? Is it so that you could ultimately know joy or peace?

That's part of it. For by knowing pain can you know the ecstasy of joy. Your soul fears not. It knows that you may have pain but it does not have to be so. The masters know that you can even experience pain without pain. You can cry from joy as well as pain. If your soul should lead you in the direction of disease you still have a choice as to how you will handle it. Do you choose to go kicking and screaming, complaining, and making everyone around you as miserable as you are? Or do you choose peace and understanding? Will you grow with knowledge? You don't have to remain ill. When your experience is complete, you can heal.

Are you saying that if someone's soul created cancer and felt subconsciously that he experienced all that he had desired he could cure himself without chemotherapy or radiation?

Yes, exactly. There have been many reported true stories of people that have been "miraculously" cured.

Well, then how do we know when we have reached the point that is the completion? When is enough? If one dies from the disease does that mean that he did not complete the experience?

The soul knows when the experience has been completed. Most times the conscious mind desires completion, but it will come about only when the soul is satisfied.

How does the mind know that?

The conscious mind knows it when the body manifests changes.

That is evident for physical healing, but what about emotional, mental, or spiritual healing?

Change can be observed when that person knows inner peace. It is a knowing and feeling of accomplishment that gives him a sense of relief, assuredness, tranquility, and growth. If he continues to open his heart and mind he will eventually remember that he is as the master—one with all creation, one with The Creator.

What advice will you give to people so that we may heal ourselves?

This book is my gift. Within its pages you will be given the answers.

Many people bring on illnesses because they don't resolve perceived problems before those issues become apparent in the physical body. When a person becomes sick, it's a positive signal because it shows him that there is a problem that goes deeper than the physical ailment. Where it is manifested in the body is an indication of what the under-lying cause may be. This book will be a lesson of how to check your self and how to deal with the issues that have presented themselves within the body.

You also asked if dying from the disease instead of healing means that one did not complete his experience. Healing is not always the ultimate result of the experience. If the soul has completed all of its intentions, then it will choose to leave the body and to return "home."

What if the life was cut short by a car wreck or a drive-by shooting, for example?

I tell you again: there are no accidents. Everything happens for a reason and with the cooperation of that soul—even if the reasons are not apparent to others or to the conscious mind.

I know that there is always a purpose for everything. What would be the benefit of being in a car wreck, murdered, or in the horrendous destruction of September 11, 2001?

The so-called victims were all volunteers to die.

Why would one wish to have such an experience?

Most people willingly volunteered out of love.

Love for whom?

They have a love for humanity and a desire to bring about awareness and change to the collective consciousness. The terrorist activity in

New York and Washington DC was to bring the result of peace, cooperation, and love to the people of the United States and the countries of the world. On a more personal level, some people choose to have a complete experience by knowing what it's like to be both one who is a perpetrator and one who is a victim at some time.

I thought that the purpose of the victims in World War II was to awaken world-wide consciousness. That doesn't appear to have happened in many parts of the world. Why would someone wish to intentionally experience hurting or killing another?

That was a purpose of World War II. It did awaken much of the world. Governments and individuals, however, still refuse to relinquish the power or the money. If the world would band together as loving brothers and sisters to share the natural resources and eliminate the illusion of superiority and domination over others, things would be improved in an instant. Another reason is that here there is only love. To truly experience what it is like to love some choose to feel its opposite, hate. Remember that one can only truly know something by knowing what it is not. If one has only been big how can he know that it is big without the comparison of little?

I know that you are a loving God and that you do not punish your children. We amply do that to ourselves. It just doesn't seem right, though, that a Hitler or a Bin Laden and their followers could kill and hurt so many and not have to answer for any of it in Heaven. I know those souls made a prior agreement, but....

No, I know that it seems to be unfair, but in reality, they did a loving thing for the collective good when viewed from another perspective.

There are a lot of people that will take exception to that statement. Many of us who have read <u>Conversations With God</u> by Neal Donald Walsh will understand what you're saying, but many will not.

That's true. There are many that will choose not to understand that statement.

Would you like to explain it for their benefit?

Okay. Before those millions of souls crossed into that life they wished to know me through faith and love in an experience. Hitler gave them the opportunity to feel true faith and to let them trust in the love I have for each soul. He and the terrorists gave people the opportunity to look beyond themselves and to band together in love and cooperation. It was an opportunity to forget color, to learn tolerance of all religions and creeds and to support and aid all those in need with a sense of love, pride, and selflessness. It was also an opportunity to test the ethics and values of each individual and nation.

In other words, they wished to test their faith by seeing if they still had faith after their memories were erased at birth.

Yes.

I hate that people blame you and rail, "How could God have let that happen?" I understand how they could feel like that. It is so much easier to blame someone else for what we have created with our hate and prejudices. The Hitlers and Bin Ladens are our reflections of those negative sentiments. I am not saying that this reflects all societies or all individuals—quite the contrary. The outpouring of love and the generosity of spirit have been exemplary in the attack on Americans. However, even within this comradery there is a segment of our population that is filled with hate and prejudice against everyone of Arab descent, even those peaceful loving people who are innocent of the atrocities.

Yes, so many forgot their intentions to experience having faith. I know how they blame me, but I love them regardless. I gave you free will and I am always going to permit every soul to experience every feeling so that I, in turn, will experience every feeling through my creations. That being my intent, why would I ever punish any of you?

I understand.

Are there any other questions?

Yes. There have been many books on illnesses within the body. What is different here?

I have given much information through many books, but what will be different here is that I'm going to make this very simplified and detailed so that everyone who chooses can begin to heal himself.

That's great, but I don't want people to think that this is a replacement for conventional medical therapy.

No, there is certainly room to work in conjunction with traditional medical treatment. If a condition has reached the point of physical manifestation and you need additional help, then get help. If you break a leg, go to your doctor and wear a cast. It would behoove you, however, to note why you broke your leg. Where do your fears lie? Why are you holding back? What is keeping you from moving forward? What is the pay-back that you are receiving either for breaking your leg or for remaining stagnant? These are some of the self-explorations that would benefit your healing. If you have not resolved the issues, what would prevent you from creating another type of injury that would indicate the same challenge or situation?

Do you not notice that people have a tendency to create patterns? People repeatedly choose the same type of partners that result in failed relationships until they are ready and willing to make changes. People hold onto their excess weight until they no longer need the reasons that initially caused them to gain it and until they are willing to make changes in their eating habits and exercise regiments. People continue to use tobacco, alcohol, and other substances as crutches for a lack of love, boredom, and peer pressure until they become a physical addiction. These patterns can be changed and there are many that are willing to facilitate these changes when a person is ready and willing to take action to become healthier. Physical or emotional change requires a change of attitude and desire and may require the inner strength of perseverance, fortitude, and patience. If your life is perfect exactly the way that you wish it to be, I congratulate you and encourage you to help others to find this paradise. If, on the other hand, you feel that you could use some improvement, here are some helpful suggestions: read this book and other books that I have inspired, take some classes, talk with knowledgeable positive people, look within, and listen to that still small voice that is your soul. You have all the answers within.

Everything is awakening to the memory of who you are. Be who you truly are. It is up to you to decide who you want to be. It is all about creation. You are creating it all. That is the secret to life and your soul's progression. It does not matter where you are at this moment but who would you like to be? You are not a human doing; you are a human being. If you are unhappy the way you are, who do you wish to be? Do you wish to be kind, loving, peaceful, thoughtful, and considerate or vengeful, grudge carrying, shallow, selfish, thoughtless, or controlling? It is your choice. Be the person that you wish to be. If you are not already that person, act as if you were that person. Act kindly, act considerately, act lovingly, and before long, you will find that you have become that person. Are you that kind of person every moment of every day or just when it pleases you to be so?

I love you regardless of your choice. I love you unconditionally. I love you eternally. I love you even when you don't love yourself. No matter what you choose I will not judge you nor punish you. That, I know, is a very difficult thing for some of you to hear. I will not condemn you to eternal damnation. Why would I ever do that to my beloved child? Where would you go? There is no such place as Hell. That is a myth that you have created. If you find yourself in such a place, it is coming from your own imagination and creation. I will always welcome you back to me in love whenever you choose to come home.

If it doesn't matter to you what we do, what is our incentive to act lovingly, morally, and ethically?

The incentive must come from the individual. Religions try to instill the desire to lead an ethical life. They build their philosophies on the teachings of my masters and messengers. What is erroneous, however, is that I will punish you if you do not follow those teachings. What are my teachings when interpreted from opposite perspectives? That is where free will enters the picture. You decide. Your growth is your responsibility. There is no time limit and no one is keeping score.

This is a book on healing. Part of that healing is accepting yourself in love as I accept you. You are your worst judge. You are the hardest disciplinarian on yourself. You create your illnesses. You create your pain. You do such damage to yourselves through your emotions and by not caring for your bodies. I created your bodies to last forever. Yes, forever. You commit suicide. You fill your lungs with smoke. Your bodies were never designed to consume alcohol. You eat animal fats and foods that are so unhealthy and put into your bodies chemicals that should never be there. It is not too late to change your habits and to make better choices. It is not too late to treat your bodies with respect and dignity. All it takes is to change your thoughts.

God, I, and I'm sure I speak for many, try doing what you suggest, but it doesn't seem to make a difference. For example, I recently had a cold in my sinuses. I tried saying affirmations to change what I believed to be the underlying reasons for the illness. I tried visualization. I even had home-made chicken soup. Whether I did anything or not, the cold was just running its course.

Yes, I know you tried to stay positive. You tried to change your thinking with daily affirmations. Underneath it all did you truly believe that your thinking alone would make a difference? Is that not your big challenge—to know, as you say, "with every fiber of your being?" This is a very simple challenge, but not very easy, unless it is.

Experientially, thus far I have tried to have that utter belief only to be let down time after time. How can we change our thinking to get such total faith?

You are on the right path. You must train your mind to accept new thoughts. Don't just say an affirmation a few times whenever you think of it. Bombard yourself with the new thought. Write it on slips of paper and put it everywhere that you are likely to see it: on your mirror, in your car, or on the refrigerator. Say it as many times as you can, aloud and with conviction. You are convincing yourself of your new thought. After you continue doing this you will begin to actually believe what you are re-training your mind to believe. It will become a knowing. That is how self-healing really works.

Many masters never doubt for one second that they will be successful in their every work. Their prayers are those of gratitude, thanking me in advance, because they have absolute faith. You, all of you, can have that absolute belief and faith, too. Each of you has it within you to do whatever it is that you desire. For truly, how can you not when you are each a part of me? The difference is that I *know* that you can. You have forgotten how powerful you are. You have forgotten that each of you is created from a portion of God. You still feel the separateness that keeps you from remembering that you, too, are a master and can perform what you call "miracles." You have forgotten that you are indeed one with all creations, one with all universes, and one with me.

Let's continue discussing my intentions in presenting this book and the two to follow. I have made myself perfectly clear through many other messengers. However, there are still so many that will listen but not hear. Therefore, it is my intention to address this book on self-healing to the populace. I am presenting it in words that are clear, concise, and so easy to understand that they cannot be misinterpreted. That they will be accepted is still up to the individual. Many in the field of conventional medicine and science will reject these writings. That the majority of readers are not in the scientific fields that would dispute these words is to their benefit. People are beginning to question prior authorities. They are no longer willing to accept the opinions of others without searching for their own truths. This is good. The job of the soul is to learn of itself and to know itself.

There is nothing new that I can tell you for you already know everything that you need to know. You already have all of the knowledge and all of the power to heal every aspect of your life that no longer serves you. Your journey is one of remembering this. I tell you this yet again: on some level you have created every aspect of your life, every situation in which you find yourself you have drawn to you, and every illness is created by you. You have created it all for the sole purpose of remembering who you are.

This book has been the result of the many pleas for help that I hear on a daily basis. In response, I send to you ways to help yourselves heal on all levels, physical, mental, emotional, and spiritual. It is up to you to choose. It is up to each and every one of you to decide if you wish to change what no longer serves you. I will not judge you either way. Hold on to the conditions that you have created or release them. Don't condemn yourselves for having created any condition. Instead, bless every creation for it has led you to where you are in this moment. Every creation serves a vital purpose.

You have reached a time in the evolution of this planet when healing has become a necessity. The beings on this planet have come to the edge when technology has worked its way to the forefront leaving behind the spirituality necessary for existence to continue. This book is being written as an answer to the cries for help from thousands who see the direction in which this planet is headed. I am making these books available so that you will be able to help yourselves. The love of God and the understanding of your relationship with God must hold us together.

So we begin. A brief reminder of history is called for so that you will be able to see the direction in which you are headed. Thousands of years ago, there was a society on this planet much more advanced than your present day society. You have your mythology about Atlantis and it is true. Atlanteans made the error of being technologically advanced without the spirituality to sustain it. Your society must change your course lest you have the same type of fate as the Atlanteans. You are growing very fast with the technology of the computer age but without the wisdom to use it properly.

That sounds so negative and scary. Can't we give a more positive outlook or at least a more encouraging one?

Yes, this book gives that positive help. I will begin by showing you how to make the changes that are necessary to heal your individual selves. By healing the individual the society will be healed. By healing the society the planet will be healed.

I will end this introduction with these words. It is up to you to decide if you truly desire to heal. Making the necessary changes might mean a big upheaval in your life. If you are willing, I will tell you this: the secret to all healing is having total belief and faith. It is absolute knowing that you can change any situation and that you can heal any condition. All of the masters knew this. I tell you this: all the healers that I have sent had absolute faith in who they were. They understood that they were a part of me. They knew without a shadow of a doubt that healing could and would be instantaneous and complete. The only difference between the masters and everyone reading or hearing these words is that you do not believe that such healing is possible for every one of you. You have but to *know* that. I present to you this book as a guide to help you.

2

Changing Your Life

When things are in a place that feels stuck it's a good indication that there is a blockage that is holding you back from attaining your wishes. At that point, you usually begin to have feelings of frustration or discouragement. This can lead to reversal of the progress you've made. I commonly hear things like, "I'm doing everything I'm being told to do. Why am I not seeing improvement? Why do life-changing experiences happen to others but not to me? Does God love that person more? I feel neglected and angry." I will address those sentiments in this chapter.

I wish to make it perfectly clear that I love every last soul. I neglect no one. How can I when you are all part of the whole that is me? I wish only the best for everyone. I truly would love it if *everyone* received his heart's desires. I never said you have to suffer. On a soul level you are responsible for all of your sufferings. This is discussed in the chapter on healing the connection with your spirit.

I never said that to advance spiritually you must give up worldly pleasures. As far as I am concerned, if it is money you wish to have, then have it. If you wish luxuries, then have them. If you prefer to lead an austere life, that's fine, too. Giving away all of your earthly possessions does not automatically make you a highly evolved soul. There are many very highly progressed souls walking the earth plane right now. Many of them are living lives of ease. Suffering isn't what I wish for anyone. Each soul makes his own choice of what he wishes to experience each lifetime.

I never said that you had to donate a particular percentage of your income to those less fortunate. Loving, caring, helping, and giving are just as important when you give of yourself. Many people only give financially to help others. That certainly is beneficial but giving of your time and energy is also important. So stop feeling any guilt if you can't donate a large financial amount. You, Love, give of yourself all the time. People benefit from your healing and teaching more than if you only made a financial contribution.

In other words, there are people living the life of luxury who are just as evolved as a Mother Theresa.

Absolutely. Caring and giving does not mean any less when it is done on a one-to-one basis. You don't have to serve the poorest masses to be as helpful. The work you do helps people that are spiritually or physically poor or are just awakening.

I don't want whoever is reading this to feel that they were just insulted.

Heavens, no. Those who are being drawn to this book are those who should be commended for wishing to help themselves. Then, in turn, they will be able to help others. I am so happy to see so many of my children becoming aware of their true power.

Part of our power is learning to help ourselves by clearing blockages. Is a blockage physical, mental, emotional, or spiritual?

It can be any or all of those. If you have a blockage, it will manifest itself by letting you feel as if you've "run up against a wall." What do you feel? It's usually fear, anger, or frustration. Fear, the basis for the other emotions, can feel paralyzing. What can you do to release the fear? As an exercise, sit down and make the following list:

1. What would your life be like should you obtain your heart's desires?

2. List your real fears associated with making life changes.

3. When you think of doing whatever it is that scares you, where does your body feel it? Look at the affected body's energy centers for the issues that may be involved.

4. If you were to remove the fear or to release the old hurts, how would it change your life? Is it changing that is your real fear?

5. What payback are you receiving by refusing to change? Why are you still holding on to your old wounds?

6. Write how you can turn change into a positive experience. Let your imagination show you the benefits associated with letting go and allowing the changes.

When you are willing and ready to make changes in your life, do this next meditative exercise:

Find a time when you will be undisturbed and go to a place of peace and quiet. You may listen to soft background music if it will help you to relax. Begin by closing your eyes and focusing on your breathing. Take several slow breaths in through your nose and exhale through your mouth. Begin at your feet and concentrate on relaxing all of your foot muscles. Work your way up the body by relaxing your muscles and letting go of any tension all the way up to the top of your head. Now take another deep breath and slowly release it. Allow yourself to feel totally relaxed.

Where is the fear located in your body? Visualize the fear, frustration, doubt, or whatever negative emotion you are feeling. Give it a shape, color, sound, taste, and smell. Make it real. Allow yourself to feel all of that emotion. What does it feel like in your body? In your mind's eye take that negative emotion and put it into large trash bags. Use as many bags as you need. Keep filling them until all the negative emotion has been collected. Then pull the bags out of that area of your body. Visualize angels, masters, or loved ones taking the bags of negativity from you, transmuting them into love, and sending them out to the universe. Really let them go and *know* that you have released your fears, frustrations, doubts, or whatever negative emotions you had.

Take additional time to make sure that you have cleaned out any residue that may remain. If you have not cleaned out any tiny remnants, they may rebuild and you will again be faced with your fears. Take your time. It may take a number of times to clear everything.

Wondering if it will work will only set you back. It is imperative that you believe with certainty that you have completely released all your fears or negative feelings. Allow yourself to feel lighter. Allow yourself to feel the relief of having released your burden. Have trust in yourself that you are healing and making a new opening for change. Trust God and give Him whatever has been holding you back. Have faith and *know* that the fear is gone.

Keep this euphoric feeling with you as you slowly return to the present to the count of three. One, allow yourself to begin to feel your physical body. Two, you are becoming awake and alert. Three, whenever you are ready, open your eyes and feel totally refreshed and wonderful.

I know that there are several releasing exercises scattered throughout this book. Would you like me to share one of the ways that I released fear?

Yes.

Okay. I felt that I needed more of a physical release. While in meditation, I began as you began. I concentrated on breathing. I started at the area where my fear resided. I allowed myself to feel the fear. I then gave the fear form. It had a color and a shape. I felt that this particular fear did not require a sound or smell. Then I began to breathe in through my nose. With each inhalation I visualized the fear being drawn upward through my body. With each exhalation I released it by blowing it out though my mouth. When the fear had worked its way up to my mouth, I could see its form leaving my body. The only thing that I had to be careful of was not getting light headed because I was working so hard to pull the fear up and blow it out.

Thank you for sharing that. You had an excellent and effective experience. Now, let's deal with the feelings of anger. Getting angry with yourself will hamper the progress that you wish to make. Stop yelling at yourself. Stop belittling yourself. Stop looking for your weaknesses. Instead, look at your strengths. See yourself as you wish to be. Stop blaming yourself for things you did or did not do. Everything that you have or have not done has brought you to this point. Do you not see how positive that is? You are reading this book. Your spirit has brought you to a place of growth. By being drawn to this book, you are being told one of two things. Either you are ready to make positive changes in your life or you have already made them and are being given an assessment of your progress. Either way, this is a positive step in an empowering direction.

Talk to yourself gently and lovingly. Thank your body for all of the things it does for you even without your conscious thought. Your heart beats, your lungs breathe, your blood flows, and you have a heating and cooling system. Cells continually replace themselves, your body naturally fights illness and injury, you think, you create, and so forth. Instead of concentrating on your aches and pains, concentrate on what you can do. Healing is affected by attitude. Be grateful to your body, your mind, and your spirit for all the things it can do and does for you every single moment of every day. Don't chastise yourself if you haven't done this before or do this infrequently. Instead, start fresh right now.

This is the first moment of the rest of your new life—no matter how old you are. Your life can change in an instant. It can be any way you would like it to be starting this minute. Each day is a new beginning; it is a clean page in your book of life. How do you wish to write your new page?

Why not start by looking into a mirror. Look directly into your eyes. Thank your spirit for all of your past experiences that have brought you to the present. Thank your body for all of the things it does for you. If your body is not in the shape or health that you desire, talk to it in quiet positive tones. Tell it that you will work with it to make constructive changes. Thank your mind for its cooperation and determination to have a positive and tenacious attitude. Don't quit! You *can* make the changes that you desire.

I would like to talk a little about negative emotions. Guilt is nothing but an off-spring of fear. What is your fear beneath the guilt? Why have you allowed another person to make you feel guilty? People can say or do anything to you but you have control over your attitude. No one can hurt you unless you allow yourself to feel hurt. No one can make you feel guilty unless you permit yourself to feel guilty. No one can make you feel angry or sad unless you allow yourself to feel angry or sad.

I know that there are times when you feel all of these emotions. It is your attitude about these emotions, however, that is important. Your feeling angry, sad, hurt, or frustrated is a blessing. These emotions can be a wonderful conduit for making changes in your life. When you are angry, sad, or frustrated enough it will inspire you to wish to make those changes. Negative emotions are a blessing because they help you to appreciate the positive emotions. Negative emotions are a blessing because they are an indication of where you can work on your path of personal growth. If you are reading these words you should commend yourself because your soul has inspired you to make positive changes in your life.

Whether you have been directed to this book out of fear or frustration or out of excitement or personal inner adventure is irrelevant. You are here now, in this moment. It does not matter what has happened in the past. You can release that which holds you to the past—whether it was five minutes ago or five centuries ago. Release any fear or negative emotion that is still draining your energy. Don't say that you can't. You *can* release anger or fear. If you won't, then that is another matter and I don't judge or condemn you for your choice. You can start fresh—right now. Just because you have had a pattern in the past does not mean that you need to repeat that pattern.

Let's talk about some areas where people find blockages. With so many of you becoming health conscious in recent years, weight has become a very pertinent subject. I'll begin by speaking to the millions of you who struggle with excess weight. You know that old patterns and beliefs must be changed. Just because you lost weight in the past and gained it back every time does not mean that this time you will gain it back again. You can do things differently now.

Begin by doing some soul searching to face your truths. It's necessary for you to understand those very good motives for your having gained extra weight and why you have retained it. It's more than you just liking food and liking to eat. There are underlying issues. Make the effort to discover your issues. This time you can release those reasons and move forward. Extra weight concerns much more than health issues. It is a method your soul uses for protection. It is a method your soul uses to hide behind your fears.

Look at your body and thank yourself for awakening the desire to make positive changes. You can do it when you release your fears and know that it is safe to release the extra insulation. You can do it when you allow yourself to truly love yourself as I do. You can do it when you let yourself feel loved. As soon as you permit yourself to heal on an emotional level then the weight will begin to lower. Releasing the fears will help to keep you from regaining the weight but to accomplish it don't eating and exercising patterns need to change, too? Be intelligent, all of you. Choose to eat healthier foods. Exercise on a regular basis. Inner work will speed the process and help to prevent the yo-yo effect.

Some of you have the opposite challenge of being too thin. You know to whom I am speaking. You try to fill your bodies with highly caloric but not necessarily healthy food to try to gain weight. Or, you find difficulty in eating. Answer these questions truthfully:

1. Why do you think your body resists?

2. What underlying fears are preventing your body from having a healthier weight?

3. Are you feeling inadequate? Are you physically manifesting feelings that you are not good enough, pretty enough, smart enough, or talented enough to be worth being more visible?

4. Is this a love or self-love issue?

5. Is this a control issue?

6. Why has your spirit chosen a body with your particular metabolism?

7. Are you are buying into your society's illusion that unless you look as thin as a toothpick you are not worth looking at? Certainly your magazines, television shows and movies illustrate that belief. Who is being hurt by your withholding nutrients that your body requires to be healthy? You forget that you are not your body. Your body is a reflection of what is really happening with your spirit. Thank your body for indicating to you your fears or perceived inadequacies.

8. Ask yourself what is really important and why is it important to you.

9. If you feel discontented how will change be beneficial?

10. What will change if you release your fears?

11. How will becoming more visible change your life?

12. Will people love you any less or respect you any less if you are a healthier weight?

13. Is that what love is to you? You have all the answers. Now it is your choice of what to do.

I know that there are many areas of concern other than health in which people find blockages. Many people feel that they are blocked in the area of finances. I keep hearing that people are stuck in a job that they hate, in a family situation that they hate, and in a life style that they hate because of their financial circumstances. You should be asking yourself:

1. Why am I really in this situation?

2. What "lessons" am I learning?

3. What payback am I receiving for remaining where I am?

Stop blaming everyone else for where you are. If it is the education you lack to move ahead, you must take the responsibility to become educated. Where do your interests lie? It is never too late to receive training and help in a new field. You made your own choices that have brought you to this point and you can make new choices to change your life. No matter where you work or what you do, there is honor in doing a job well and to the best of your abilities.

What about those of you who have been trained and cannot seem to find a job that is acceptable in your area of expertise? This has been a common complaint. Many of you feel that you have settled into a position in which you feel unhappy because you require the money to have a roof over your head and to give you sustenance. Granted, there has been a great shift in the job market in recent years. Many businesses have become defunct. The political climate has also created big shifts in the job market. Consider this. The door is closed but by opening a window, even if it is a temporary window, those people that are in a seemingly dissatisfactory position are gaining new experiences, new incites, and new relationships that would not have been afforded them had they stayed in their preferred field. When they do find a desired position they can enter into it more rounded, more appreciative, and more empathetic to others.

My Children, what comes to you really comes from you. Why is it that some people seem to find their perfect job almost immediately and other people never seem to find contentment with their work situation? Look to your belief system. Do you really believe that the perfect job is just waiting for you and you have but to apply? Expect that to happen. Know it will happen. Believe it and it will come to pass. If your spirit has directed you to a temporary position away from your area of expertise know that there is a very good reason for that. Learn from it. Take advantage of it and grow. Take the lemons and make lemonade. By whining and complaining you are creating or re-creating the negative experience.

Create what you desire. Picture the perfect job. Make it as real as possible. Be very specific as to the details. Make it like a motion picture with you as the star. See your self applying for that job or creating that job as an entrepreneur. See yourself being accepted and making the salary you wish to have. See yourself going to that office, salon, or place of business. What does the building or room look like? What does it feel like to get or to create that job? Feel the elation or contentment. Use your senses. What does the work place smell like? What sounds are apparent? If it is food related, can you taste the food? What do the objects around you feel like to the touch? Pick a time frame for this position to come into reality. Put all of your desires, wishes, and creations into a bubble. See this bubble coming out of your body from the solar plexus, the third eye area, or your heart area. Blow the bubble out to the universe and watch it as it floats farther and farther away. Once you have sent it out, expect it to happen just as you are creating it. Don't keep asking or sending it out. That only indicates that you are doubtful and don't really expect it to happen.

Pay attention. An opportunity may be right in front of you, but if your eyes are closed you won't see it. It may not come exactly as you envisioned. It may be better. Put pictures around you that remind you of your manifestation. Keep a positive and knowing attitude. It can be fun to see how quickly you can create things and bring them into your reality.

Life does not have to be difficult—or it can be. You choose. I know what you are going to ask. What about all those people in homeless situations or in third world countries that barely have enough sustenance let alone work? I repeat it yet again. There are no accidents. Each soul has chosen his situation for whatever he has desired to experience for his own purposes. By all means help your fellow mankind but keep in mind that on a soul level each has freely chosen his agenda. Be a catalyst for change—if that is the desire of the other person. It is not your place, however, to make choices for another. (You know that I am not including someone who does not have the mental competency to make decisions.) The most caring thing that you can do for another is to encourage him to make his own choices.

Parents, help your children to become independent and responsible adults. They came to you to have certain experiences. If, when they reach adulthood, you do not let them live and take responsibility for their own lives you are hampering their growth. I know that parents don't want to see their children hurting themselves. Don't, however, force your opinions on your adult children. You may encourage them to see what they are doing and to makes some changes. Ultimately, though, I have given each person free will. Be loving, be supportive, be encouraging, and be silent unless asked. Isn't it enough to be responsible for your own soul, your own lessons, and your own growth without trying to run someone else's life? You chose your life and the things that you wished to experience. Try to remember that your child is another fully developed soul and made his choices, too.

3

Letting Go of Physical and Emotional Bonds

I have some advice for you on letting go of old thought patterns. You don't have control over all situations sometimes because of the choices of others and sometimes because you are drawn to a circumstance. Your challenge is to change your thought patterns of how you react to those situations that you deem to be negative. In reality, all situations have positive valuable when viewed from another perspective. By examining the negative, it affords the opportunity to observe the positive. Negativity gives insight as to where there is work to be done and can inspire growth. When viewed in that light every opportunity becomes a magnificent experience.

Thus it is with healing. By understanding your ability to create you understand that you may also change that creation. Most of you are walking around in a state of unconsciousness. You don't take responsibility and are unaware that on some level it is you who control your life experiences. There are those of you who are beginning to awaken. It is no accident that you are reading this book. Your soul has brought you to this point.

I will offer to you simple clear-cut suggestions for changing the patterns that no longer serve you. The easiest solution has been presented to you over and over. Some of you hear it. Others only listen. You tell yourself that you can follow my suggestions and you do so, for a minute or two. I tell you this: the patterns that you have formed were not formed over a minute or two. They took days, weeks, months, and even years to be cemented into your daily behavior. Do you really expect to change these patterns in only a few minutes if you happen to think about it? There are those of you who can make changes instantly, but for the majority of you, your belief system has been that change takes time. So, if you sincerely desire to change a habit or thought pattern, it will take some conscious effort on your part.

Look at what you have created. Know why you have chosen to repeat the pattern. If it no longer serves you, decide what changes you wish to make. Really listen to the words that come out of your mouth. Are you denigrating yourself even in jest? Your subconscious mind doesn't differentiate between good and bad. Each thought, each word you say to yourself and about yourself is registered within. When you think to do it you say a positive affirmation. Then you countermand it in the next breath. You tell yourself, for example, that you are releasing your excess weight and becoming thin and healthy. In the next minute, however, you are joking about being fat or unhealthy. I know that you make jokes as a self-protection mechanism, but your subconscious mind does not know that. It only hears what you say about yourself. All of you must stop the entire negative self-talk and thoughts if you truly desire to heal.

For the benefit of those who have not heard my dissertation on this, I would like to expound a bit on how your creations come into fruition. Everything begins with a thought. You do not realize just how powerful your thoughts are. They are the living energies that give birth to creation. If you find that your thoughts are not serving your desires, change those thoughts. To do this you must become aware.

The first step is to pay attention to what is in your mind. Re-mind yourself to change your thought patterns. This will take conscious observation on your part. If you perceive that a negative thought has crossed your mind, change it. Cancel that thought and turn it around to a positive thought.

The second step is to speak your thoughts aloud. State your intentions verbally as much as possible. Talk to yourself out loud when you look into your mirror in the morning. Speak your intentions while driving in the car. Tell a friend or a family member. Keep talking to yourself and reaffirming your new thought about yourself. Don't just do this once; do it a thousand times during the day. The more you do this, the faster a new thought pattern will form and the faster your new creation will be realized.

The third step is to put your new thoughts into action. If your creation is to be a healthier thinner you, act upon your new thoughts. Choose food that will be healthier for your body and, dare I say it,—exercise. You know the things to do that will bring your new creation into being.

I realize that old thoughts may have a great influence upon what you are trying to change. You may have suffered as a child or even in a past lifetime and made a promise to yourself that things would be different the next time around. Are those old promises still serving your present needs? Why are you still holding on to those old hurts? Are you using old wounds as an excuse to avoid change? So you ask, "How do I know if my efforts are being thwarted by a past promise I made to myself?" The answer is simple. You have all answers within you, everything you have ever thought or done. You have within you the ability to recall any of this information. Have you not heard of listening to the "still small voice" within? It is your own voice that carries all of the answers. At the same time is it not my voice also, for are we not one and the same? Throughout this book are suggestions for accessing inner knowledge.

Let's talk about letting go of physical and emotional conditions. Most of you haven't been aware of the fact that you are ultimately responsible for your condition and it is up to you to consciously choose to release it. Let's begin by asking why you originally created your condition. Are your real motives challenging your faith, looking for inner strength, seeking inner peace, being a teacher for others, or, perhaps, are control or love issues involved? The answer will come with introspection, by examining your life. Be totally honest with yourself even if the answer is not one the conscious mind wishes to hear. Remember that your soul knows why you are in this condition.

Once the true purpose of the creation has been revealed look to see why you are holding on to the condition. Ask yourself:

1. What need is still being fulfilled? The ego fills its own needs.

2. Are you receiving added attention? Why do you need to receive the attention?

3. Do you control those around you by your need? Is it the only control you have in your life? If you allow others to control you, is disease a way to maintain some life control? Only you know the real reason for holding on.

4. Is this an emotional crutch that you use? Is there not another way for you to soothe your emotions?

5. Is fear stopping you? Why are you so afraid to release the condition?

6. What would change in your life should you be healthy and independent?

7. Are you so fearful of change?

8. Are you afraid of being open to search your inner feelings? Are you afraid to see the true nature of your being, of seeing who you truly are?

These are things that must be answered.

In your conversations with Walsh you tell us that need is only an illusion. Yet here you are telling us to find what we think we need. This sounds contradictory.

Yes, need is the greatest illusion upon which most of you have based your lives. I do discuss this extensively in his book. However, I would like to say a few things about that here. The truth is that I need nothing. I am everything already. You, being a part of me, a part of the whole, need nothing, too. That's right, you require nothing. You do not even require air to breathe. You are eternal and cannot die. You have forgotten who you are. You are not your body. Your body serves you. You live life after life with different bodies. Indeed, you do not even require a body for your soul to live. You choose to incarnate to have different experiences.

Your first misconception is that I require something from you. Indeed, you have created stories substantiating this myth. In doing so you have created another illusion—that of separateness from me. With this separateness you imagine that now you, too, have needs. Most of you are still clinging to this false illusion that there are things that you do need. Until you awaken to the point of remembering the truth, we speak to you on the level at which you can relate. So, you think that you have needs? Identify what you think you need.

Thanks, God.

You're welcome.

Once you have determined the payback of why you have held onto the condition, see how letting go will affect your life. Don't be afraid to imagine how life would change. Think of your future as a healthy independent person. You can still maintain a healthy relationship—or can you? Is your relationship with another built on need? Would it collapse if your life changed? Is it worth keeping yourself emotionally or physically crippled in order to maintain a particular relationship? These are important questions to contemplate.

If you have satisfied yourself that you are ready to release what you have created, then it is time to consider your next step. I would recommend that you begin by taking some private time alone. Look into the mirror. Look into your eyes and sincerely thank yourself for having created the condition. It served a very good purpose. Perhaps it protected or insulated you. Perhaps it taught you some valuable lesson. Perhaps it let you concentrate on other important issues. Perhaps it gave you a new perspective on the difficulties of life in the physical form. Perhaps it taught you tolerance for others. There are always benefits. Whether your condition has been painful or not, whether it has been physical or emotional, whether it has been of long duration or short, thank yourself sincerely for having given you such a valuable experience.

Now that you have shown yourself the appreciation that you deserve it is time to begin work on actually releasing whatever condition is causing your distress. Let's use a meditation:

Sit quietly in a comfortable seat and close your eyes. Concentrate on allowing your body to completely relax. Scan your body for any areas that may be holding tension. Focus on relaxing those areas. Let the relaxation flow over you like waves. Allow yourself to sink deeper and deeper into comfort.

If you have a physical ailment or depression due to a chemical imbalance, picture a large computer screen in front of you. See yourself on the screen. See your ailment displayed on or inside your body. What does your ailment look like? What would it take to correct the condition? Use your computer mouse. Be imaginative. You may use any tools or method to fix the physical ailment. All tools or help that you require are on icons at the bottom of the screen. Take your time. If there is a painful area, see it as red. Use your mouse to strip away the red and to fill that area with a brilliant white-gold light. Fill it again with a healing blue or green light. See your body completely healed and healthy. See yourself unrestricted and meeting any physical challenge you wish. You have become the picture on the screen. Use your imagination.

The mind is so powerful. You are so powerful. Know that it truly is within you to have the strength that you need to realize this healing. See yourself as you wish to be. Completely put yourself into the picture. Make it real. Can you hear yourself laughing? Can you feel yourself lighter and freer? What does it feel like to feel joyful? What does it feel like to feel strong? Feel the energy and the revitalization of being a strong, healthy, complete person. If these are feelings that you have not felt in a long time search your memory for some incident or kind word that made you feel happiness. Try to re-create that feeling.

Know deep in your soul that you are making this happen. The door has been opened for some dramatic changes. You are creating the changes that will be this new picture. If this is what you truly desire, know that it is within your capability to make it happen.

You will bring yourself back to the present on the count of three. One, begin to feel your body back in your seat. Two, you are becoming more aware and alert. You are beginning to feel the excitement of knowing that you have made some real changes. Three, whenever you are ready, opening your eyes, smiling, and feeling wonderful.

I would like to address those people for whom visualization in meditation seems difficult. Some of you are better at sensing things, hearing things, or feeling things. Use whichever method is the best for you. Perhaps you feel that you cannot "see" a condition within yourself but you can sense that something is not quite right. Try to sense in what area in the body there may be dis-ease. Allow yourself to feel what that feels like. Whenever you think of a particular challenge you may be facing, do you get a stomach ache or a headache? Make note of the area of the body that is being affected. What are the true issues behind your discomfort? Describe what it feels like. Does it feel like a big empty space? Does it feel heavy or tight? Perhaps you can hear your body talking to you. Perhaps it tells you that you are getting an ulcer or that you should see your doctor about getting an antibiotic. Use your intuition to sense when things have reached the point of physical manifestation. If medication will help to ease your discomfort, then use it. However, do not neglect the investigation as to the underlying cause for the ailment.

If your condition has been emotional, take some time to think about the following questions:

1. If a relationship inspires you to feel sad, what would it be like with two independent people that are together happily by choice?

2. If the relationship were built solely on need, what would it be like without that need? Perhaps it is time to move on and release that relationship.

3. What would your life look like without that person?

4. What would your life look like without someone else controlling you?

5. Are you held to that person out of guilt? Why do you feel guilty? Why do you let them make you feel guilty?

6. Why are you afraid? Guilt is an outgrowth of fear.

7. What would your life look like if you stopped accepting the guilt or the fear?

Ask yourself questions about whatever area of your life feels unsettled. Is it physical, emotional, mental, job related, financial, or people oriented? You can change your situation. It doesn't have to be hard. Many let go of their conditions easily because letting go is only difficult if you make it difficult.

Happily, it is almost impossible today to turn on the television set or to read a newspaper without seeing a show or an article about miracles that have happened to someone. Does it appear that miracles only happen to special people? Of course it doesn't. So called "miracles" are happening every day to thousands of ordinary people just like you. Many of these miracles happen just by taking control of your own life.

Conventional medicine has had such control and influence for so long that it is pleasing to see people finally taking control of their own health issues. I am not saying that medical help is not necessary. In so many cases ailments have progressed to such an extent that traditional medicine can certainly aid in healing the condition. Such wonderful strides have been made in delicate and non-invasive surgeries. What medicine has not done is to heal the underlying issues that originally caused the affliction. So I ask you, why do you let things grow to the point of needing outside medical help? Would it not be healthier and faster not to let your emotional conditions fester and build to where they manifest physically? My advice to you would be to make the time and effort to work out what is bothering you. Don't let it reach the point of physical disease. If you feel "stuck" in your efforts, there is no stigma to receiving the outside help of a psychiatrist, psychologist, or hypnotherapist.

Trust your instincts. If they tell you to get help, then get help. Your soul knows what is best for you. Release the anger and rage if that is what you are holding before it begins "eating away at you." Refuse to accept guilt that another is trying to foist upon you. Stop pitying yourself and do something about changing your life. If receiving or giving pity no longer serves a purpose in your life let it go. Of course you can feel empathy for another person, but is holding onto pity really helping them or you? These are serious matters for you to think about.

Now let's talk about the benefit of clearing anger, pain, fear, or guilt. The mind is a wonderful instrument for self-protection. When a person has been injured in body, mind, or emotion, the mechanism of the mind puts up a screen that allows him to conveniently forget such a pain. The mind forgets but the injuries are imbedded in the actual DNA at the time of the injury. In order to complete the healing it is important to clear out the blockages that have been created. I am referring to emotional pain and blockages. I am not talking about memories that were erased of physical pain after a physical trauma. It is the emotional traumas that prevent people from moving forward.

We will deal with clearing each area beginning with anger. This is sometimes a difficult area to clear because many times it is clouded by denial. For example, it is difficult for many people to admit that their parent or guardian would actually harm them. They carry an underlying anger that they push farther and farther inside themselves. Eventually it begins to manifest itself by "eating away" at them with illnesses such as cancer or ulcers. So, in order to maintain health, it is important to release that anger.

There are several methods that I will recommend for dissolving anger. Many people find it very helpful to write in a journal. Let your mind think back to your childhood. Allow it to free-associate. Trust yourself to write down any memories or thoughts that come to mind. Forgotten incidents and thoughts may appear if you change your writing patterns and write with the opposite hand. You may surprise yourself with what comes to the forefront. Memories from your earliest childhood rise like hidden springs bubbling from great depths and breaking at last onto the surface of your mind. Small forgotten incidents have indelibly imprinted themselves and, when added together, have created patterns in your life that now need to be released so that new healthier patterns may be established.

Many times writing a letter to the person or persons who have hurt you will release much anger. Take as much time as you need. Write as long a letter as necessary. Include everything from your earliest memory that has hurt you or angered you. Spare no words or feelings. When you have *completely* released every emotion and said everything that you have always wanted to say, sign the letter.

Then we will do a little ceremony. Take the letter and tear it up into little pieces. Burn the pieces in a fireplace, ashtray, or any safe place. Gather up the ashes and bury them. As you bury them, state your intention to release all the anger and hurt contained in the ashes. Bury this portion of your past and let it go. Allow yourself to feel freer and lighter knowing that you have released the burdens that have been as a weight around your heart.

Sometimes the anger or rage has become so intense that just writing in a journal or writing a letter is not enough to release it. Sometimes it takes a physical action to release that anger. Here is a recommendation for you: when you are alone, go to your room and put a picture of that person (or picture them in your mind's eye) on your pillow. Some people use a punching bag. State aloud that it is your intention to release the anger within yourself. It is not your intention to hurt anyone else. Call my angels or me and we will help you.

Then really let yourself release all of your pent-up anger at that person. Yell, scream, cry, curse, hit the pillow that represents that person, pound the pillow against the bed, and do whatever it takes to physically release your anger. Sometimes it takes several repeated sessions to really let go of all of your rage. You may feel drained after the first session, but repeat it the next day or the next. Sometimes there is residual anger that you didn't know was still there. You will know when you have completely cleared everything. Then allow yourself to feel the peace that comes when you have truly let go of your emotional burdens. Sleep or rest. It can take tremendous emotional as well as physical energy to release deep anger and pain.

Let's take a few moments to talk about the little hurts. People many times say thoughtless hurtful things. Much of the time, they do not even realize that they have hurt you because you say nothing and internalize the pain. You replay the hurt over and over in your thoughts and it builds over a period of days or weeks or longer. So begins the process over again.

What I suggest to you is to change the pattern. This time don't let the pain internalize. Try to respond within twenty-four hours. Talk quietly and calmly to that person. Don't attack (either verbally or physically) the one who hurt you, but tell him that what he said was hurtful. Try to make amends with that person. Then just let it go. Each time you replay the hurt in your mind you are giving away your energy to that person. Is it really worth it to you to give them your energy? It will clear better if you can talk it out with that person. If you feel that you cannot talk face to face write it in a letter.

I would like to continue by talking about letting go of childhood pain. As I previously indicated, some hurts are imbedded so deeply that the mind has created amnesia to numb the pain. This has been a wonderful method of self-preservation, but it eventually needs to be cleared to maintain a healthy body, mind, and spirit. Are there not times when you just feel the need to cry or you feel "blue" but you really don't know why? Chances are very good that there is a child or even an adult within you from your past that is crying. Any number of tiny things like a smell, a song, or a picture can trigger a feeling. They can even trigger a physical response like a rash, sneezing, or pain.

The answers can always be found within. Go into a relaxed state and ask that whoever is crying within you appear before you in your mind's eye. It could be an inner baby, child, teenager, or adult. You are the one in control. You are there only as an observer and, as such, are perfectly safe and secure. When that inner person appears always be very gentle with him. Never yell or scold him. Speak quietly and lovingly to him. Introduce yourself saying that you are your future self and you know that there is something that is bothering him. Urge that inner person to tell you what is hurting him. Help him to correct the situation. If he is missing a loved one that has died, in your meditation call in that loved one to spend a little time with both of you. If there are words that were left unsaid this is your opportunity to have a dialogue with that person.

If your inner person is hurt because of damage that had been inflicted upon him do whatever it takes to correct that situation. In your meditation or mind, go with him as a protector, a mediator, or an ally. Call in angels and call in your higher spirit. Call in anyone and everyone that you wish to accompany you. Then call in the perpetrator and tell him exactly how you feel. Make sure that you assure your inner person that he is completely safe now and that nothing can ever hurt him again. You are there to protect him. You can even take a magic wand or a weapon into your meditation for his protection. In your imagination you can change whatever happened to make it have a happy ending.

It could be that your inner child is just missing you. Spend some time with him in your meditation. Play with him on the swings or go to the beach or where ever you used to feel safe and happy. When you are ready to come back to the present give your inner person a hug.

Tell him that you love him, and tell him that you will visit him again if he needs you.

If it seems difficult to find your inner children ask for the assistance of a hypnotherapist or a psychotherapist. When you have cleared away the sadness of your past you will feel as if a huge emotional weight has been lifted from you. If this has been affecting your physical weight you may even find pounds being released. You can talk to your inner beings as to why you have been holding onto excess weight. No matter what the situation I tell you again: you already have all of the answers within you.

Let's turn to some thoughts on fear because it is your fears that restrict you. What is actually happening is your reluctance to make the changes necessary to affect the healing process. In other words, you resist the condition that you have created, thereby drawing it to you yet again. What you resist persists. What you fear you draw to you. It is part of a "law of attraction." You say that you are creating a grand circle, and indeed you are. You have been begging me to help you to break out of this circle. I say to you this: you can leave this circle in an instant if you so choose. To do this would require you to change your thoughts. That may take some discipline on your part.

If you have created a disease you hold it to you by your resistance of it. Refrain from continually dwelling on it. There is great power in thoughts and words. Do you wish to continue to give the condition more power and energy? Instead of complaining and cursing it bless it. For by not resisting, by accepting each occurrence and finding the blessing within it, does healing pour forth. Seek within to find the positive experience that you have created. By changing your perspective you will begin to heal your condition.

Would you please give us an example that would clarify "what you resist persists?"

Okay. Let's say that you repeatedly injure yourself enough to keep you either on crutches, pain ridden, or bandaged. There is a part of your being that creates this physical handicap because your fears have "immobilized you." By refusing to deal with and eliminating those fears you continue to re-create excuses that keep you from moving forward. So your spirit says, "This lifetime you wanted to learn "whatever." You've been avoiding doing what you need to do because you are afraid of the changes that it will bring or of the work required to learn this. It's time to roll up your sleeves and to face the fear. The harder you have fought to avoid doing this the more you have hurt yourself." Your higher spirit or your spiritual forces will continue putting you into situations that will enable you to have the opportunity to deal with it and to move past it. When you finally stop resisting, when you bless the fear because it is showing you what you wish to learn, and when you stop hiding behind pain you'll begin to heal.

Some people choose to avoid dealing with pain or fear by numbing themselves with alcohol or drugs. Some people choose to use these toxins as a means of acceptance or image projection. Let's talk about changing addictions. When you fill your bodies with toxic chemicals like alcohol, drugs, or tobacco, the body sets up a chemical reaction that creates a desire followed by a physical need for that chemical. You still have a choice and the ability to help yourself. Go to a detoxification program. Let counselors, doctors, friends, or others who have released the chemical help you. It may be a challenge to resist falling back into the habit of using that substance, but if your desire is strong enough it is so much healthier to resist. We are not criticizing or judging you, but merely making suggestions. When will you take responsibility for your actions? Stop blaming your youth, your friends, your past, or your spouse. You chose to light up that cigarette or to take that drink. I know that at times we angels seem idealistic. We have never experienced what it feels like to crave drugs. We do, however, see what it does to the body, the mind, and the spirit. So we do encourage you to clean out the toxins. We realize it may not be easy, but it is worth the effort. You are worth the effort.

4

Letting Go of Spiritual Bonds

The majority of spiritual blockages stem from religious beliefs that have been implanted during one's childhood. Many religions paint a picture of God as someone to fear and as a separate being who sits in heaven looking down on each person, judging, and keeping score. Many are taught that unless you are "good God fearing people" you will burn in Hell. You are taught that you are sinful even at birth because of the sins of your forefathers. When you are in pain you try to make deals with God. You promise that if God lets so and so live or heal you will give up all your bad habits, go to church regularly, or call your mother every week. If your friend or family member should die you blame God. I've been a good (fill in the blank). Why did God take my child, father, or friend from me? You think that God is punishing you or you give up on God. You feel that there is no God or there is a vengeful God.

It is sad to see the psychological damage that people do in my name. For many people, this is the spiritual challenge that you created in your blueprint before you came to this lifetime. You need to reach a point where you begin to question your childhood teachings. I would like to set you straight on a few points.

I love each and every one of you. I created each of you from a part of myself and love all of my creations as I love myself. Each and every one of you, no matter how you were raised, no matter what you have done this lifetime or what you believe, is deserving of my love. No one is more deserving of my love than is another. I see all. I know all. Nothing you think or do is hidden from me. How can it be hidden? You are a part of me and I am a part of you. Even if you have committed what society deems as sinful or wrong I still love you no matter what. Now, this is not to say that I am giving you permission to go around murdering and hurting your fellow human beings. That is something that you must leave to your own conscience. I have given free will to people. If you choose a maleficent path, that is your choice. You will not burn in hell. There is no "hell." When you finish this lifetime and return home I will not judge you. You will find that you are a much harder judge on yourself. There are still many who have not found the path of light and love once they have finished their earthly sojourn. I have not abandoned them. They have abandoned me. Help is always available to them if they will but accept it.

I would speak, also, about the issue of making deals. I do not deal and I do not take your loved ones from you. If they "die" it is entirely of their own choosing. Each person makes his own blueprint before coming to his lifetime. He chooses the "lessons" that he wishes to experience and he chooses when and how he will leave this lifetime. I realize that it is painful when a loved one dies. Even those of you who truly know that only your loved one's body is gone but that his spirit is still around you feel pain and must go through the grieving process. I ask, however, that you respect the right of that person to choose to leave when and how he wishes.

I know that you are thinking about those people who fight to live but whose bodies are so disease ridden that they fail. There are many that feel guilty that they have brought these conditions upon themselves. I say to you that there is no reason to feel guilty. No, your conscious mind probably would not choose to die a painful or diseased death. Yes, you may have been able to prevent much of your condition by changing your thought patterns and releasing harmful attitudes and habits. Stop feeling guilty. Everything happens for very good reasons on a soul level. It does not happen because you think "sinful" thoughts or use the wrong crystal. That is nonsense. It can, however, be affected by maintaining a positive attitude and an absolute belief system. If your loved one is still struggling to live, even on his deathbed, know that it is mostly fear that is holding him back. Death is not to be feared; it is only another transition. I may add that it is a much easier transition than that of the birthing process. It is so joyous here where everything around you is love and beautiful, vibrant, and more alive than on your earth plane. There are many accounts of "near death" experiences to substantiate this description.

Let's continue by discussing how the psyche works. So many of you are stuck thinking that the conscious mind is all you need to control your life. Actually, it is the subconscious mind with which you should be working. How do you affect the subconscious mind? You can do this by simple repetition of positive affirmations. The subconscious mind takes into it everything that you hear, see, taste, smell, touch, or think. It does not judge right from wrong, good from bad, or up from down. It is like a personal computer that takes in everything and stores it. You feed your computer so much negativity every single day. You are not even aware of the half of it. Every time you turn on the news reports, read the newspaper, listen to gossip, look into the mirror and criticize yourself, or allow yourself to be belittled at work that is feeding negativity into the computer of your mind. Every time you hear thoughts from your childhood running through your mind like: "you're not good enough, smart enough, pretty enough, too fat or too skinny, bad at math, can't do that because it is not a woman's job, or you are too stupid to go to college" it reinforces those negative faulty thoughts in your computer. Every time you catch yourself hearing one of those thoughts consciously change it into a positive thought. Yes, you are good enough and smart enough, and you can do anything you set your mind to do.

You just do not realize how powerful your thoughts are. You are so careless with your thoughts. People here think a thought and it is made real immediately. Should they wish to travel across the country they have but to think it and they are there. Needless to say they are very careful with thoughts. Can you imagine what it would be like to have your every thought manifested immediately? The masters have learned to do just that. How many of you are as loving, kind, considerate, and thoughtful as to be able to wield that much power? You do not even love yourselves enough to handle it let alone being able to affect those around you. How judgmental would you be? It is not your place to control, to judge, or to decide anyone else's life. You seem to have enough problems managing your own lives.

Parents have the job of caring for and guiding their children's lives until they are responsible enough to be independent. However, you are just a caretaker for that child. It is not your child. It is my child. It is your job to love it and to help it to know and to love itself. It has its own agenda or blueprint to follow and you must love it enough to let it be independent and to follow the path that it has set forth for itself while remaining there to be supportive and loving. You must concentrate on changing and improving your own life. By changing your inner world you change the world around you. Life does not happen to you; it happens from you.

There is a universal law of attraction that I mentioned earlier. What vibrations you send out are what you will attract back to you. If you are positive, loving, and caring that is what you will draw into your life. If you are negative, stressful, and fearful that is what will be drawn to you. You also draw to you those people who demonstrate character traits that reflect the things within yourself that you might wish to examine. Try to relax, to pray, and to let go and believe. The more "up-tight" you feel and the more fearful you are the harder it will be for you.

I would like to continue with releasing spiritual bonds that hold you back from achieving your fondest wishes. Beginning with your earliest teachings as a child think back to your first recollections of what your parents or guardians taught you about God and religion. For many of you this alone will be a challenge because your minds have effectively blocked out much of your early experiences. Therefore, I will recommend some ways to refresh your memory. Begin by writing in a journal. Once you have started, you will surprise yourselves at the memories that will appear in your notebook. Some of you can release old memories while in meditation. Command your mind to show you scenes from your childhood. Others of you would do well with the aid of a hypnotherapist. He will be able to take you back even as far as your experiences before birth and in the womb. It may surprise you to know that the attitude of your parents about your forthcoming birth can influence your present thoughts.

The faulty thinking that you may have been taught through the guise of religion can affect many areas of your present life. Certainly, your views on morality will have been influenced. How you feel about marriage, pre-marital sex, sex in general, homosexuality, abortion, capital punishment, abuse, your relationship with God, and your relationships in general, and many more issues have been influenced by your religious or non-religious early upbringing.

Are your parents' or spiritual counselors' teachings restricting you from living a full life? Were you taught that sex is a sin? Have you completely gone the other way, perhaps, and given yourself freely to sex without any emotional commitment? Why do you do the things that you do? Do you find it necessary to use drugs to make it through the day? Why do you rely so heavily on artificial stimulants to bring you awareness and joy? Can you not see the beauty of my creations as stimulants around you? Why do you not feel that they are enough to nourish your soul? For that matter, why do you not feel that *you* are enough to nourish your soul? Each and every one of you is a beautiful miraculous creation in your own right. Why do you let the opinions of others make you feel inferior and unworthy? Why do you feel that anyone else's opinions are any better than your own? You are just as important as anyone else. You are just as loveable. You are just as worthy. You are just as deserving. Just because you do not make as much money, are not as physically pretty (by who's standards?), or do not have a job that is deemed important does not mean that you are any less valuable as anyone else.

Take each issue individually. What were you taught from your earliest recollections by your parents, grand parents, spiritual counselors, teachers, and friends? Yes, even your childhood peers have influenced your thinking by what they were taught by their parents. As adults, you think that you have become independent thinkers, but have you? Do you hear your parent's, teachers', or minister's voices coming out of your mouths? Are you teaching your children exactly what and how your parents taught you? They were only teaching you the way in which they had been taught. Does that still serve you now? Why do you think that their methods are the best? Remember that each of you has your own bond directly with me and you know the truth with a capital "T" in your own heart and soul. Some of you just need a little reminder of that.

You have wonderful powers of observation. Observe the kind of person that has resulted from those old teachings. Is this the kind of person you wish to be or the kind of people you wish your children to be? Do you always act lovingly, kindly, and considerately? Are you happy with your life? The masters are. Each and every one of you can be a master if that is your desire, regardless of your chronological age or physical state. Why not begin now at this very moment?

Start by letting go of any thoughts or traditions that are no longer serving you. Does this make you feel fearful? Do you fear that by being a truly independent thinker you will break the bonds of family relationships? If your family members truly love you they will still love you whether you agree with them or not. Is it a requirement to love someone in your family just because they are related? Why have you chosen to be in that family? Remember that when making your blueprint before you reincarnated you chose the family circumstances that would give you the experiences you wished to have.

Sometimes you choose to be with family members because of a love or friendship tie, but other times, you choose to be with family members to experience "lessons." As an adult have you had those experiences? What have you learned from them? Can you put it past you yet?

Do you still not realize that you can let go of the old faulty thinking and see the truth for what it is? I realize that letting go of the past can be scary because it means stepping forward into an uncertain future. Sometimes, however, it's necessary to take a leap of faith knowing that never are you alone. Trust that things always happen for the best even though they may be challenging while you are in the midst of them. Trust that you will always be in the right place at the right time for the right reasons.

I am not purporting that you break the bonds of family or friendship, but sometimes it may behoove you to let go of people or ideas that are no longer serving a loving or useful purpose in your life. Bless them and release them. If the connections are very important to you then keep them. Why must you permit what they tell you to influence your life? They have a right to their own beliefs and thoughts, but you do not have to agree with them or let them control you. You have just as much a right to your own beliefs and thoughts. You are just as valuable a person in every way.

Those of you who are reading this book have been drawn to it because you are consciously trying to advance your evolution. You are mostly adults now. As an adult I would like you to look at your life objectively. You are no longer the child that is used to being told what to do or what to think. You are an independent being as well as being a part of the greater whole. You are each a different part of me. You seek different experiences. You have different thoughts. There are no two of you that are exactly alike. That is how I created you so that I could have myriad experiences of all types through you.

I would like to close this chapter with some final words about letting go. I am not going to tell you what to do. It is for you to decide what to hold onto and what to release. There is no time limit to what changes you wish to make. Your soul cannot die; it merely makes transitions to another form. You may have as many lifetimes as you wish to experience everything that you desire. It is for you to choose the kind of person you wish to be. It is for you to choose the kind of lifetimes you wish to have. It is for you to advance your own evolution at your own rate of speed.

I love *all* of your experiences for each has its own merits. I would never condemn you nor punish you. However, I am happy to advise you for I know that that is one of the things that brought you to this book. If you really wish to make positive changes in your life then take control of your own life. Keep a positive attitude. Talk lovingly, frequently, and daily to yourself. Visualize your life as you wish it to be. *Believe* that you *can* produce positive life changes. *Know* with your whole being that you *can* accomplish your desires. You are not alone; I am always with you. I love you and am happy to send to you all the encouragement that you need.

5

The Importance of Belief

The most important aspect of healing, whether it is for you or others, is the mind-set of absolute belief of the healer as well as the acceptance of the recipient. I know that this is an area that can be of great challenge especially when one is trying to heal oneself. Many times a person will say that he has done whatever he has been told to do or read about doing in books but does not appear to be healing. The answer to this is simplistic but not necessarily simple. Methods like visualization, praying, meditation, or self-talks are effective. However, the reason that complete and possibly instantaneous healing has not taken place is either because he did not have the faith that he really *could* heal himself or he was not completely ready to receive healing.

How does one achieve this total belief? Let us look to acceptance of our innate abilities. God created each person by taking a portion of His/Her energy and fashioning a spirit or soul from this energy. Each creation is a bit of God. Therefore, does it not make sense that each soul has some of the abilities of The Creator? Because God can heal anything instantly does it not make sense that each person who has the inclination to heal has the innate ability to do so? Today, many people are finding that they are quite effective using healing methods like Reiki, Therapeutic Touch, or faith healing. What is the difference between these healing methods and those used by so-called "miracle" healers? The difference is that the masters have a total and absolute faith in that each person has the ability to be healed. These healers merely awaken the memory of the "God" within that person. You have only to know with total conviction that you *are* a portion of God and that you *have* the abilities that you require. This is a knowing of your whole being, not just your intellect.

The acceptance of the person to be healed must also be taken into consideration. Many people may say that they wish to heal, and consciously, yes they do. However, subconsciously, there may be reasons why they are not ready to accept the healing at a soul level. Remember that people create their own diseases, if not on a conscious level, at a soul level. Their reasons are quite valid. There may be reasons for continuing their dis-ease. Maybe it is a way for them to receive the attention they crave. Maybe they have control issues and by creating their disease or condition it is a way for them to control others. Or perhaps, by using their body, it is the only way that they have any control at all. There are times when a soul will create a condition as a spiritual challenge. Perhaps it requires a test of personal abilities or perhaps the disease will bring him the faith in God that his soul feels it would wish to experience. There are so many reasons people create their physical conditions.

Mental conditions are also created for many reasons. Sometimes when a spirit is planning his future life he plans a challenge such as depression. When that spirit chooses the body and life to come he may choose a body that will have a propensity towards a brain that will occasionally go out of chemical balance. It may be his challenge to learn how to deal with the mood swings. He may choose to correct the imbalances with drugs or he may choose to learn to work through the periods of imbalance. It depends why he has chosen this challenge. What has he chosen to experience? That is why you are on the earth plane. Many of you call these experiences life's "lessons." If that is how you wish to view them, then that is fine.

We on the other side of the veil are always here and always happy to assist you in your efforts. However, there are some challenges that you must face on your own. If you have chosen a challenge such as "absolute belief" in your own abilities no one but you can learn that belief. We will encourage you, we will cheer you on, we will give you suggestions, we will applaud your progress, but we cannot give you belief. This you must do on your own. We understand how frustrated you feel. We hear you when you feel like you are on a merry-go-round and don't know how to get off. You say that you would have this absolute belief if you could just see yourself doing instant healing. However, without that absolute belief it is impossible to do it. So it is like a circle. If you could see it you would believe it. However, you won't see it unless you first believe it. Around you go. It is such a conundrum. That brings us back to the question of how to learn to believe.

More often than not people make a request for aid in healing. They pray, they cry, and they harangue, but when it is not forthcoming they lose their faith. What they don't realize is that their pleadings were only wishes and their belief in their actually healing is what has been blocking that which they most desire. When you ask for help with healing we hear. We would be most happy to assist with it if it is appropriate to do so. Once it has been requested, however, do not keep petitioning because that says you don't truly believe that you have been heard or that you will heal. Once you have asked, place your trust in us and believe that healing will be forthcoming. Then let it go.

May we please have an analogy?

For example: God hears each and every prayer. When you ask for something He logs it into His computer, figuratively speaking. When the same request is logged in again the computer says, "This has already been entered." So it won't compute. Instead, it says, "This person must have more practice dealing with this issue until he learns to work through this and until he believes that this issue can be released."

It seems to me that that is creating a circle of frustration. We are wishing and praying so hard to be rid of a condition but by continued praying are re-creating it each time. That hardly seems fair.

No, we know it is not what you consider to be fair, but never-the-less it is how things work. It's like sending your children to school and trusting that the teacher will teach them what they need to learn. You don't put them onto the school bus then follow them to school. You don't sit in the classroom and tell the teacher what to do. It's a trust issue. This is the same. Pray or do what you need to do. Trust that your prayers have been heard and that you've done your utmost. Then let it go and know that things will work out for your highest good.

You said that most times prayers are answered. Sometimes they are not. How can we trust when there are times when prayers are not answered? How or why should we believe when there are times when that trust appears broken?

That is a very good question. Yes, there are times when prayers are seemingly not answered. We say to you that God truly does hear each and every prayer. There are times, though, when it really is in your best interest to work things out by yourself. We will always support you. We will always love you. We will always encourage you. However, we will not help you when it is in your best interest to work things out by yourself. Sometimes God's answers are not the ones that you want to hear. Don't ask the question unless you are really willing and ready to hear the answer.

Why should we keep praying when we think we won't receive help?

Keep praying because it is strength. Most people need that strength of knowing that even in your darkest moments you are never abandoned or alone. Dear, we both know how frustrated people are because they feel overwhelmed. However, repeated praying over the same issue will only bring on more frustration. Once again the key is belief. Pray. Know that things will be as they should and let it go.

You're asking us to have an unlimited unquestioning faith. That is unreasonable if we are disappointed repeatedly.

I understand exactly what you are saying. In that premise it would seem to be somewhat of an unreasonable request. You need to remember that in most case scenarios help is given. Only on occasion is it withheld. Even then, though, is it not of help just to know you are not alone and you are truly loved? Although at times you must meet your challenges by yourself we still help by doing what we can. We clear whatever we can for you. We whisper encouragement into your ears.

We cheer you on and applaud you when you complete each step of the journey.

That's fine, but most people can't see you applauding. They can't hear your words of encouragement. They can't feel your hugs. Most of us don't know when you are around us. We can't use our five senses to know of your presence. Do most people have that much of an unflappable faith?

Most people do not. That is why they turn to religions. For most people following the rules of religions and working in a religious framework reinforces belief in the Creator. Praying reinforces belief.

It is when people need God the most that they pray and sometimes feel that they have been abandoned.

That's true. Religions remind you that you have not been abandoned. I know what is coming next. You are going to talk about people turning away from organized religions because they are realizing that many of the man-made rules no longer fit their needs.

You must be psychic.

Maybe I am. Yes, religions could use some changes to fit these times.

It's a can of worms to open that topic.

Yes, let's stick to this book on healing and love. Healing does require belief and self-love.

I would like to continue by discussing how belief affects the total being. Human beings are created like onions; they consist of many layers. Picture if you will, the physical person in the center of the page. Obviously, this is the part of your being that you see when you look into a mirror. This is the part on which the majority of people focus. It is the physical body that is the indicator through pain or pleasure of what is happening in your inner world. Talking to your physical body and working with it to keep it healthy aids your inner growth. It shows you the areas of your life that require attention. If you have pain or discomfort in a particular area of the body look to see the issues that are generally found in that area or in that energy center and how they are applicable to your situation. Pain can be a blessing and a wake-up call so pay attention to it. Be sensible. Don't try to analyze every little thing. I am not referring to the pain of a paper cut or a stubbed toe because you weren't paying attention to your walking. I am talking about chronic pain or an injury that lasts over a period of time. Your body shows you whether your life is in balance.

Surrounding the physical body is the etheric body. This is the energy field or aura that surrounds a person. Your scientific equipment can detect this energy field and special cameras and equipment can photograph it. Cameras can even detect the many colors incorporated in the auric field. When someone has concerns about an issue the colors in the etheric body start to change.

The etheric field has a direct impact upon the physical body; it feeds the physical body with energy. When you are tired it is the etheric field that must re-energize and replenish the body. It works through the immune system to help fight disease within the physical body. This is where diseases begin. When tears or holes appear in the etheric body energy leaks out and disease can begin forming in the physical body. For example, if you feel a headache coming on you sense it first in this energetic body.

There are many healers today that work with the etheric body either by feeling or sensing this energy field or even by actually seeing tears as dark spots. This is the theory on which practitioners of therapeutic touch (a healing method being taught in some nursing schools) operate. Patients can physically feel the calming effect or energizing of this energy field. Because of the sensitivity of the etheric body healers must be careful when working with a patient. For example, if someone comes into the area of the head too quickly he can actually cause the patient to have a headache.

Have you not heard that occasionally, if a person loses an arm or leg he still feels what is called "phantom pain" in the etheric body? It feels to him as if he still has that limb. Kurlian photographs taken of the area of missing limbs have actually shown outlines of those limbs as still in place.

Around the etheric body is the astral or emotional body. This is where one feels the fluxing of emotions. This is where you feel divine delight, fun, happiness, the pain of conditional love, hurt, joy, betrayal, or anger. The astral body houses love, family, and relationships. It is here that you must deal with your inner children, your past, and your insecurities. It is in this area that you must have total belief. You must learn to trust your feelings. When you trust you experience the joy and the peace that come. It is here that you must release your anger, your rage, and your fear before it works its way down through your etheric body and into your physical body.

Repressed emotions, either pain or fear, affect peptides or receptors that open the cells. This is where your psychosomatic illnesses originate. For example, if you feel very angry it bursts a hole in the etheric layer and energy begins to leak out. If the anger is not released it can eventually work its way into the physical body as disease. Stress that is allowed to build can eventually manifest in the body as ulcers or many other conditions.

There are times when your astral body so impacts your etheric body as to be readily visible to those who are able to see colors in the auric field. It is your emotions that can change those colors. There are many books available that can interpret what each of the colors indicates.

We are happy to see that in the last fifteen to twenty years there has been a surge of greater understanding and openness with regard to healing the emotions. People finally understand the impact that the emotions have on the physical level. Psychology, psychiatry, and hypnotherapy had its beginnings much earlier, but it was not as understood, appreciated for its value on physical healing, or practiced to the extent it is today.

Around the astral body is the mental body. The mental body is more than just the mind. The mental body encompasses all of your thoughts. Thoughts "pop into your mind" seemingly at random. You often feel that you have no control over your thoughts and that they just come "with a mind of their own." What you do have control over is when a thought that is negative or hurtful comes into your mind, you can, by paying attention to that thought, change it to a positive and beneficial thought. The mental body houses all of your thoughts.

Your mind is more concerned with the present thoughts. If you have a dilemma you ponder the solutions in your mind. You replay situations over and over. You worry and imagine various scenarios that could happen. You build the possibilities until they become blown out of proportion in your mind. If you would just let it be and stay "out of your mind" the solution will present itself. You will find that most of the things about which you worry never come to pass into reality. It is the mental "body" that will bring you the solution. Relax and allow yourself just to be with the problem. Perhaps you will receive the answer in a dream or in the relaxed state just upon awakening or falling asleep. Some of the most prolific minds on your planet find that if they take a short "cat nap" the solution to a problem presents itself in that relaxed state. The mental body incorporates the mind but encompasses more.

The mental body is often at war with the emotional body. It is the mental level that keeps disease popular because the mind does not always respect the emotional needs of the person. The mind often suppresses what emotions try to come forth. When you feel upset the mind tries to justify it and saps energy from the etheric body leaving the physical body feeling tired.

May we have an example here, please?

Okay. You are concerned with weight and its effects on the health of a person so let's take a food situation. You (any person) feel upset or sad. Your emotional body says, "I'm really upset and I want some comfort food. Give me chocolate—and I want it now!" Then your mental body steps in and says, "You can't have chocolate. We're trying to lose weight. Chocolate will only add calories. You'll be sorry later when you step on the scale." Your emotional level will start to whine and so the battle begins. Is this beginning to sound familiar? Sometimes the emotional body will win and you will choose instant gratification. Sometimes the mental level will win by reasoning out the entire situation.

The mental body that incorporates the mind decides the thoughts that are brought through the astral body, through the etheric body, and into the physical body. The mind in the physical body is not just in the brain; it is actually in all of the cells. Each of your cells has its own memory. Thoughts and incidents can be imprinted into a cell memory within your DNA. There have been many examples of seemingly inexplicable pains or cravings that a person experiences after having received a transplant. There are many stories of transplant recipients having dreams, memories, or desires of the person who donated the organ. Don't let this stop you from being an organ donor. This does not happen in most cases.

Whether your thoughts are negative or positive has a great impact on all of your layers. We suggest that you make an effort to be vigilant of your thoughts and attitude if you wish to remain healthy.

In other words thoughts actually originate in the mental body, pass through the astral and etheric bodies, and reside in the physical cells that are "the mind."

Correct.

Above the mental body lies the ego consciousness. It is the ego that occasionally gets you into trouble because it is the ego that plays tricks with your mind. Love, sometimes you complain to us that you are not sure if you are hearing us correctly or if a thought is coming from somewhere in your mind. I will tell you that ninety-nine percent of the time you hear us very clearly. That last one-percent is when the ego steps in and tells you things that you wish to hear. It is your ego that lies and plays tricks with your mind. I am not just speaking directly to you. Almost all people are in the same situation and most have an ego that takes over the mind much more frequently than yours.

How do you tell the difference between our words to you and thoughts that are coming through your own mind? Use your intuition and feelings. You know when something *feels* right. Sometimes things you say or write are stated differently than the way you usually state them or use vocabulary that you generally don't use. Sometimes things come out that seem to be completely new information. When we write we have to go through your filters (as is true with everyone we use as messengers). Look at the information coming through. Sometimes it is very familiar to you, but sometimes does it not seem to be new? Is this not true also for the general population that is reading this book? Are there not times when you have been speaking and when you have finished wondered, "Where did that come from?" Occasionally do we not put the words in your mouth that will comfort a friend or help to find a solution to a problem?

Do you really think that you are completely alone in your world? I tell you this: you are not. Just because you cannot see us or do not think that you hear us does not mean that we are not around you. In truth it is easier for us to communicate through your subconscious and supra-conscious mind than to speak with your conscious mind. We are happy that so many of you are learning to listen and to trust us even when you don't hear us directly. You use us by paying attention to your feelings and intuition.

I have learned that if you say, "Turn left," I don't question, I turn left. I know that it is in my best interests to do so. You've literally saved my life on a number of occasions. I know that you whisper things into my ear and it comes through to me as intuition. I've learned that I always regret it when I don't listen to my feelings. Thank you.

Above the ego is the spiritual body that is your connection to the Divine. This is where you know the Truth with a capital "T." Your soul or spirit has the total belief in you and your path because it is still connected to the Divine. Even if your conscious mind has forgotten your mission, your soul has not forgotten and it already has absolute belief.

As you peel away the layers and filter down toward your energetic bodies, that absolute belief can begin to dissipate. It is in your "mental body" that you begin to lose your belief. You analyze and in doing so begin to rationalize that if you cannot use your five senses things cannot be proven to be "real." The western world has become so technologically minded that you think that unless something can be scientifically proven it has no validity. You make things so much harder on yourselves when you follow that line of thinking. Some of you who have chosen to be true existentialists have it the hardest because you have removed yourselves from God. That is your choice and we do not criticize nor judge you. By your choice it may be that belief in yourself and in your abilities is strengthened.

Please note here that the speaker has changed for the subsequent writing.

I would like to say how powerful the mind truly is. Dear ones, you can talk yourselves into and out of almost anything. Haven't you noticed that loving yourself is a real key to healing? Do you not know that is the answer to your soul's yearning? Let's talk about self-love. What do I mean precisely? Self-love does not mean loving what you see in your mirror. So many of you see the physical image and think that if you like what you see there that means you like yourself. That lasts about thirty seconds. "I look great…except for my thighs, wrinkles, a pimple, or my hair isn't perfect." What will it matter if you see an attribute that you consider to be a flaw? Will your loved ones love you any less? Will your colleagues or peers respect you any less? Of course not because it is your spirit they see.

Will you not see that your body is perfect just as you are? I created each and every body perfectly for the purpose of having a home for the spirit while it is on the earth plane. Every body is the perfect body for the spirit that inhabits it for the duration of that life. You decided the body type that would be the most useful for you whether it is tall, short, skinny, fat, beautiful, plain, athletic, or crippled. Every body serves the purpose I intended. Every body serves the purpose of its inhabitant. The body that you pre-selected has the genes that your spirit may use to fulfill its mission. So be grateful for your body because it is doing exactly what it should be doing for your spirit, yes, even if it is quadriplegic.

What about the illnesses you create? Do you not know that this, too, is part of your master plan? Some illnesses are pre-planned before you even come to have your lifetime. The others are created by your soul to give you the experiences you requested.

So, if everyone around you has a disease and it is not in your agenda you won't get it.

That is correct. Now, how does this correspond to belief?

<u>First</u>, you must truly believe that you are in the body that you chose. Stop wishing for something that you are not. If you are truly unhappy with many of your attributes you have the free will to change them. Dye your hair, change the style, wear colored contact lenses, or lose or gain weight. Those things truly are not important but if they help you to feel better about yourself then do it.

<u>Second</u>, believe in you. That is what is important. Know who you are. I have created you and I always create beautiful and wonderful beings—what you call miraculous beings. You have spinal cords that support you, organs that act as cooling and heating systems, lungs that breathe, organs that function without your giving them a second thought, hands that hold and nurture, brains that think and create, and on and on. Yet you let a blemish or part that may not be as perfectly formed or functioning as another be your focal point. Well, stop it. Thank your body for all the wonderful things it does for you. Appreciate what you have. If your body is not in the condition you would like remember that there are reasons and very good reasons for this. For example, if you are over-weight thank your body for protecting you. Fat is insulation, a protection and security. In many cases it represents a substitute for what you feel as a lack of love.

Love can be a complicated issue. True self-love is doing what is in the best interest for your highest good. If it is truly in your best emotional interest at certain times to equate love with food then eat because it fills a temporary need. Now here is where self-love comes in. If you feel you must eat it is within your free will to choose your food (unless you are somewhere that food is prepared for you without your input). You can choose food that will maintain better health for your body.

Somehow celery just doesn't seem like a comfort food.

So eat the chocolate. You can always choose to exercise later to burn off the calories.

<u>Third</u>, you must believe that what you do can truly impact your own health. So many of you have placed your body in the hands of others and feel no obligation for your own state of wellness. Yes, doctors can fix up a situation. However, it is your responsibility to learn why you created it and what you can do to remedy the true cause of it. Too many of you will look to anything but your own responsibility. I am not chastising you, punishing you, or criticizing you. I am merely commenting on that which is observable. You blame the weather, germs floating around, or a tree that stepped in front of you to trip you. Look where you are going. Rest your body when it tells you it is tired. Feed your body when it says it is hungry. Take care of your body. Do you forget to protect it? Make it last. Bodies were created to last so much longer than yours do. In reality they really could last centuries, but you do not care for them properly. You bake them in the sun. You feed them unhealthy foods. You fill them with smoke and drugs. You do not protect them sufficiently for weather conditions. You over-work your bodies, put stress and strain on them, and then you expect them to continue to work perfectly for you. My dear Children, look at what you do to yourselves. Learn to love yourselves, to respect your bodies, and to appreciate them. When you have caused dis-ease within them know that you have it within your power to assuage the situations. BELIEVE. You are so powerful within yourselves.

If you need help, get help. I have sent many messengers and many masters to give you the help you seek. What do you do but reject them as crazy or foolish. Yes, there are those among you who have set themselves as my messengers. There is greed and power that entices such actions. They are not my ministers but ministers of their own making. Those that choose to follow have their soul's "lessons" to learn. Use your intuition to guide you. Look with your eyes wide open and hear with open ears. You will know the truth. My messengers speak with loving hearts. My masters heal with love. If a person who claims to be a master tells you that you must do things his way and believe as he does, beware. A true master knows that you have all the answers within yourselves and he will encourage you to listen to your own inner voice.

Now for you messengers and masters and for all of you loving spirits who open your hearts to healing, teaching, and helping others: stop feeling guilty with regard to receiving monetary compensation. Why do you feel that everyone else may receive payment for sharing his gifts but you must give freely? Look at whom you are paying. Is it all right to pay drug dealers and prostitutes? Is it okay to pay a fortune to people for throwing a ball or reciting written words? Yet you will not reward a teacher who gives of himself to help you create or a healer who helps you toward health? Such diversity in payments seems rather unbalanced does it not? Because a minister heals the spirit why isn't he paid as a doctor that heals the body? If one lays hands upon another to aid in healing why is that any less a gift than an artist creating a painting or a musician a beautiful symphony?

Now let's talk about belief in me. I know that the majority of people believe in me. They call me by many names. They pray to me through my creations. However, they do not truly believe that we are one and the same. They see me as a separate being to pray to at a distance. To know me truly is to know yourselves for you are part of me. Does this not tell you how much I love each and every creation? Coming from the whole does it not tell you that each of you is just as important as the next? Why would I create one race of beings or one type of human being better than the next? I am all beings, all colors, all nationalities, and all creeds. Why would you feel superior or inferior to your neighbor knowing that you all come from one being? I created differences so that I could experience what those differences felt like. There is no better or worse; there is only different. Yes, each of you is different, a different aspect of me. You are like those round crystal balls with many facets that you like to hang in your windows. We are all as one crystal and each of you is a facet that shines its rainbows on everything it touches. You are my beautiful crystal lights and colors.

Some of you have forgotten this. Some of you wish to experience what the absence of light and beauty is in order to know that light. For how can you truly know the light and beauty without its opposite? By what means do you have to experience it but by comparison? I leave that thought with you.

Belief is really a knowing that you are in essence God. You are a part of me and how could I love any part of me more or less? Do you love your right hand more than you love your left hand? As I love myself I love each of you.

If you would but know you are God you could heal everything. You could do everything. You are everything. Do you not believe that I can heal anything? Does it not make sense that because you are my energy you can heal everything you have created? So know we are one and take that knowledge to unchain the "God" within yourself. Take our love and light and share it with your other parts—your brothers and sisters. More importantly take responsibility for your own selves. Look what you do to yourselves. Please stop criticizing and judging yourselves. Find and use your individual gifts and talents. Learn to truly love and appreciate who you are.

6

Healing the Connection to Your Spirit

Many people find that they have a difficult time in healing their physical body because the mind, the body, and the spirit feel somewhat separated.

The spirit always stays near the body, doesn't it?

Yes, it does. Putting yourself as an example—your spirit is always about six feet above your head. You are always aware of your spirit. You call her for private talks and there are times when you have even argued with her. Most people are not as aware of their spirit. They don't know the relationship that exists. I'll tell them. Each person has a spirit that is his or her connection to God. The spirit is the part of him that stays in both worlds and completely knows his every thought and every deed. Who that person truly is lies within his spirit.

When a person "astral" travels it is his spirit that does the traveling.

Is that what you mean by the spirit being split off?

In reality the spirit can never totally leave the person for as long as he remains in the physical world. It is attached by a silver cord that is severed when he "dies." Few people consider their spirit as a separate aspect of themselves. While you are in the physical the spirit works as somewhat an independent person while at the same time maintaining its connection. The spirit draws circumstances to you. The spirit leads you to where you need to go and brings to you the people with whom you need to associate. However, you still consider your mind and body to be your primary bosses. Am I confusing you?

Not at all, but I could see where some readers would be confused.

Because most people do not even think about their spirit or rarely do it can occasionally feel as if you are somewhat splintered. Are there not times when you feel you are "falling apart?" That is when you must "pull yourself together." Call together all the separate parts of you (those discussed in the chapter on belief). Let's do a little meditation that will help to make you feel whole.

Find a quiet comfortable place. Put on some soft music if you wish. Allow your body to completely relax. Allow your eyes to close. Concentrate on slow breathing in through your nose and out through your mouth. Focus on relaxing all of your muscles from head to toe. Begin by relaxing your scalp, your facial muscles, and relaxing your jaw. Let go of all the tension you may be carrying in your neck and shoulders. Just let your arms relax all the way to your finger tips. Breathe peace and comfort into your chest and lungs. As you exhale let go of any stress or cares. Relax your whole torso. Let go of any tension or anxiety in your back. Relax your stomach, your hips, and your buttocks. Let the relaxation flow down your legs and all the way down to your toes.

Now visualize yourself sitting or standing with balls of light dancing around you. Each ball is a different color. One colored ball represents your spirit. Perhaps it is a shinning gold or a deep violet. Another ball represents your mind. It may be a lovely indigo color. One ball represents your emotional self, another is your ego, and another represents your energetic self.

There are smaller balls of colored light also flitting around you. They represent your positive attributes. One beautiful ball may indicate your being a responsible person. Another may represent your honesty. Each ball is a reflection of your personal attributes. See all of the beautifully colored shining balls, each representing a different aspect of you, floating all around you.

Then on the count of three pull all of the colored balls inside of your body. Picture them all drawn into you like you are a magnet. One–two–three. See all the colors mingling and mixing within you. As the colors mix see yourself becoming a brilliant white being. You are completely filled and surrounded by a brilliant white light. As you know white is the combination of all colors.

Feel yourself as a whole being complete in every aspect strong, secure, and in control of your self. Instruct yourself that at any time in the future you feel you are splintering or "falling apart" you have only to snap your fingers and immediately you will "pull yourself together." Allow yourself to feel the power within you. You know that you are complete in every way. You are perfect exactly as you are. You are God's perfect and beautiful creation and God loves you exactly as you are—no matter what.

Stop feeling that you need to act perfectly. Stop feeling that you are inadequate in any way. I tell you that you are perfect exactly as you are. You have the strength within you to accomplish anything that you wish to do. You are a whole, powerful, beautiful person. Believe in yourself and know that you can create your life exactly as you wish.

At the count of five, you will awaken feeling strong, healthy, powerful, capable, and ready to accomplish anything. One, feeling yourself back in your seat, two, three, beginning to feel feelings in your hands and feet, four, moving your neck and becoming more aware, awake, and alert, and five, whenever you are ready, opening your eyes, feeling completely refreshed, energized, and ready for wonderful new adventures.

I would like to talk to you today about healing and your spirit. In reality your spirit does not really require healing. What do need healing are your attitude, your thoughts, and your ego. Your spirit is just fine because it is your connection with home, heaven, or whatever you wish to call "here." Your spirit cannot be harmed. Your spirit is filled with my unending and unconditional love. When someone feels "dis-spirited" about something it is his thoughts or emotions that are interfering. Know that it is all right to feel "blue." If you are having a low day let yourself have a pity party. How long it lasts is up to you. You can choose to whine and complain. You can choose to be grumpy and self-pitying for as long as you wish. I wouldn't recommend it for more than a short while unless you choose to be a hermit. Do you enjoy being around people that are always negative? Do you enjoy being around people that continually whine and complain? Wouldn't you rather surround yourself with people who are cheerful, happy, and have a positive outlook? Why inflict your negative self on others?

Remember that I created a law of attraction. You will draw to you people with similar vibrations. You will also draw to you people and situations that will help you to learn what you wish to learn—to experience that which you wish to experience. People complain that they repeatedly have failed relationships with the same type of partner. You will keep drawing to you people that will help you to learn your lessons. If you have let others control or abuse you, you may change by learning to assert yourself, to honor your own desires, and to realize that you are just as important in worth as anyone else. Your thoughts and ideas are just as valid as another's.

Perhaps your lesson is to learn independence, to recognize your self-worth, to learn to be responsible for your own actions, or to defend your thoughts. If you have been the one to hold the reins of power perhaps your "lesson" is to respect the thoughts or physical being of another, to wield your power with kindness, understanding, and compassion, to see the value in your fellow humans, or to realize that there is no superiority.

When you have finally "had enough" you will make the changes necessary to break away from your old patterns. Whatever is your agenda when you are truly ready to make those changes in your life you will notice that the people who have fed your old patterns will begin to leave your life. The only way that they can remain is if they, too, decide to make the changes in their life that will enable you to stay together. I am not saying that the loss of some of these relationships will not be painful. Indeed, they may feel very painful. Know, however, that these changes are for your highest good and that you will begin to draw to you relationships that will benefit your new patterns. Try to remain positive. Know that you are making changes that will help you to be a stronger, more confident, and healthier person.

How do we make changes in our lives?

Begin by realizing that it is important to become aware that on some level it is you who create all within the framework of your life and it is within your power to heal and to change. It is simple really. It begins with a change in thinking. Why have you created your situation? You already have the answer.

How does one access the answers? This is done by listening to that "still small voice" within for therein lie all of the answers. A simple way is by going to a quiet and peaceful place where you know that you will not be disturbed. Close your eyes. Take some deep breaths. Ask your mind to give you the answers. Your mind will show you a sentence or a picture. Or, you may hear a voice within giving you the answers. You may even sense the answer. Some people find answers in contemplation while walking a labyrinth or sitting by the ocean. Go wherever you find solitude and peace. If you cannot receive the answer immediately don't be frustrated. Ask it again another time. Ask for the answer to come in a dream. Ask for the answer to come any way that it will. Then pay attention. The answer may come delayed.

If you are having difficulty receiving answers you can still help yourself to alleviate physical discomfort. Allow your mind to visualize the part of the body that is being afflicted. In your mind's eye see the problem area. If it is painful you may see it surrounded in red. In your mind's eye strip away the red. When all of the red is completely gone see the area as a blank space. Visualize a brilliant white-golden light like the sun coming down from the heavens and completely filling that space. Now picture a healing light of blue or green coming down within the white light and fill that area with healing light.

Remember that healing is not limited to holistic methods. Who do you think inspired the person that discovered aspirin? You can take two aspirin *and* call me in the morning, noon, or night.

I love your sense of humor.

Thank you. Humor is one of my best creations.

Why do you not always receive an immediate answer? What is it that is blocking you from change? The answer is simple, but it is something that most of you seem to find difficult to accomplish. You must relax and you must believe. To use the common vernacular you become very "uptight" about your situation. It is continually plaguing your thoughts and building a condition of stress within your system. If you do not learn how to relax the stress will eventually become manifested within your physical body and thus compound your complaints.

Has the stress or emotional pain you have been feeling already realized itself physically? Ask yourself the question again, "Why have I truly created this physical condition? What is the origin of the dis-ease or of the irritation that has become evident within my physical body?" It is much easier to run to the doctor's office and to receive a pill or diagnosis from a doctor, but this does not get to the root cause of the disease within the body. It is not our intention to put modern medicine out of business and medication does take care of the symptom, but that is not enough. It is essential to find the underlying issues that are being physically exhibited.

I know that it can be difficult not to become over-whelmed and anxious when your thoughts are consumed with fear or pain, be it physical or emotional. I tell you this: If you would learn to relax, and I mean your mind as well as your body, you would find it much easier to cope on a daily basis and to heal. I suggest to you that you do whatever will help you to relax. Allow your mind and your body to release all thoughts and tensions and allow yourself to be completely in the present moment. Breathe. Take deep breaths slowly in through your nose and completely fill your body with oxygen. Then slowly release your breath through your mouth and consciously let go of any tension with each exhalation. Meditate, take a bath, walk in the sunshine, do yoga, or swing in a hammock.

Mentally put yourself in a bubble and fill that bubble with anything that makes you feel happy and calm. Do not allow yourself to think about any problems or concerns that you have. Doing this once or twice a day will readily help your well being and will alleviate much stress. You will find that it will be much easier to deal with the causes of your anxiety when you have learned to relax.

Many people receive their answers in dreams. If you are one of these people, before you fall asleep, ask your mind to release to you the information you require. Keep a pad of paper and pen at your bedside. Immediately upon awakening, write down your dream. Many answers can also be found in the altered state just before sleep or upon awakening.

So now you have the answers.

The first step in making life changes is to take responsibility for the situation in which you find yourself. I know that many people today recognize their responsibility. I frequently hear, "God, I know I have brought on this condition. I have done everything the books tell me to do. I meditate, I visualize, I pray, I have changed my diet, I exercise, and I've been manifesting like I've been taught. Why am I still ill? Why am I still in this condition? Why isn't my body cooperating? Why isn't my marriage better? Why isn't the money coming in? Why can't I find a job? Why can't I find someone who will appreciate me?" On and on continue the questions.

I see that people are trying very hard to change the situations which they believe make them unhappy. There are several things to take into consideration here.

One: the soul has brought on these conditions for very good reasons. It is for the conscious mind to figure out what those reasons are. It is not enough, though, just to know the reasons. It is the soul, the true spirit of that person, who knows exactly what that person wished to experience, why he chose that particular challenge or "lesson" as so many of you call it, and when it feels satisfied that the experience has been completed.

Two: the conscious mind finally reaches a point when it feels that it has had enough. It feels frustrated or depressed. It feels that it has finally reached "the end of the rope." That is when you will read a "self-help" book, attend a lecture, or try whatever methods offer a glimmer of hope that you will be able to bring about a change in your situation. Yet, the conditions appear to remain constant.

The second step, and perhaps the most important key to change, is belief. It sounds very simple to say but you must *believe* that you *can* heal yourself and that your situation *can* change. The mind is extremely powerful and thoughts are truly things. The mind can heal. The mind creates but the mind can also undo. If you doubt you won't be able to create that which you seek.

I understand that this can seem very complex for you. I am asked, "How does one obtain this absolute belief?" In order to do so it is necessary to be aware of your thoughts. Make a conscious effort to control them. Make the effort to stay positive. Repetition is a key factor here. Keep telling yourself that you can heal yourself. You can change. Frequent repetition of thoughts will turn them into a belief. Each and every one of you has the ability to heal and to change that which you have created. Know that you can do that. Do it with all of your heart and every fiber of your being. Know that you are a powerful being. Many of you seem to have forgotten this and need to relearn to love yourselves as well as others. Therein lays the entire secret.

Step three is to remember who you are. My Children, you have forgotten that we are truly one. By your separateness you have created your illnesses, your wars, your hatred, your feelings of superiority or power, and any other of the ills of the planet. Many of you intellectually or socially may agree that all are one, but emotionally you have not accepted our oneness. You see differences between you and your neighbors. You see differences in life styles, colors, creeds, and beliefs. You compare your social and financial status with the next person and that leads to feelings of superiority or inferiority. You use your money or your gifts to make you feel more powerful, more intelligent, or stronger than others. You like feeling different and special.

Like each snowflake or drop of water you *are* each unique and special with your individual gifts and talents. However, those differences are just that—differences. It is not a question of better than, only different than. You think that your way is the only "right" way, but there are many "right" ways depending upon one's perspective. It takes all of those individual and unique droplets of water to make up the whole that is the ocean.

If you truly accepted the fact that we are all one, that no one is better than another, and that I love every one of my creations unconditionally, there would be no more wars, no more poverty, and no more illness. What, then, would be your purpose for returning to the earth plane? Your purpose is to remember who you are. You have but to awaken the "God" within yourselves and know that you can truly heal yourselves as well as to help others to heal.

You say that you believe in me but you do not believe in that part of me that is you. You go to your place of worship and pray to me as if I were a separate being. Indeed, some religions teach a further separation by having an intermediary like a priest, Jesus, or a saint pray to me for you. When you are in trouble do you not call on my divine aid? Do you not talk to me out of your loneliness and your fear? Do you not thank me for the beauty that surrounds you and when wonderful things happen? Yet, you forget that you are a part of me. You can create "miracles," too. You must have faith and *know* that you have that innate ability. You must know with absolute conviction that healing or change is taking place.

The difference between the majority of the population and the masters that seemingly heal instantaneously is that they know with absolute certainty that each person is connected and has the ability to heal. The master knows that he is the "sum" of God. Your religions translated that to be the "son" of God. You are all my sons and daughters. Together you make up the sum of God. Know your oneness with the all and your life will change quickly. If everyone knew his connectedness the planet would change in an instant. There would be no more murder, no more rape, no more cheating or lying, and no more "holier than thou." You are all as holy as thou. When you know your self-worth and when you learn to love yourself you will be ready to make changes in your life.

To reiterate and to capsulize:

1.   Take responsibility for your own life.

2.   Know with certainty that you are powerful and can make changes.

3.   Know that we are all one.

4.   Love yourself.

7

Handling Frustrations

I would like to discuss how to handle frustrations. Many times people do the work required to heal but quickly undo all the work. They make the time to release anger or fear, they write in journals, and they sit and really think about their lives and what changes they would like to make. They talk themselves into making changes in their lives then talk themselves right out of those changes.

When you are truly ready to make changes do the work required and trust that those changes are taking place. Keep repeating positive affirmations to reinforce your belief. Occasionally, you may see what appears to be a step backward in your progress. In reality, this is not a reversal. It is merely a test of your resolution. To continue forward toward your goal in the face of renewed challenge shows strength of your conviction. Of course you may experience feelings of frustration at times. I know that sometimes it feels over-whelming to you. However, it is precisely at these times that you must roll up your sleeves and exert more effort.

What really frustrates me is when I do the work, but there is a time delay in the results. It's very disheartening not to see any immediate changes and even what appears to be the worsening of a condition. How do we know that we have truly changed a situation in the face of unseen progress?

This is where faith steps in. You begin by asking for change. You think about it, you fantasize about it, and you dream about it.

The first step towards creation is thought, but it is just wishing at this point.

75

The next step is belief that you really can create that which you wish to have. Believe in yourself and your own abilities. Believe that you can make the changes necessary for creation. Repeat your affirmations loudly, frequently, and with conviction. Visualize that which you wish to have. Put pictures of it all over your home as a constant reminder of what you are creating. Belief, however, is not the final step to creation.

The final step is faith. Belief takes you most of the way there, but it is faith that takes you to the end. Faith is an absolute knowing. Faith leaves no room for doubt of any kind. When you have this absolute faith and conviction anything is possible. The frustration of most people is that you mostly believe in your ability to create the changes that you would like to have in your life. However, there is still that little bit of doubt that you can completely do it. You take the necessary steps but you put your faith in the numbers. In other words, you believe only what you can see.

Okay. So please tell us how we can believe that change is really taking place when the standard indicators of physical change are not apparent? How do we combat this frustration?

My dear ones, I do understand your frustration. I know that to tell you to have faith in your abilities is something that most of you find to be very difficult. I understand how hard it is for you to do the work and to close your eyes to the physical indicators. That, however, is actually what I am asking you to do. Because most of you still feel separate from me you do not remember how powerful you really are. When masters perform what you call "miracles" they *know* that we are working together. You—yes, each and every one of you, are just as powerful, just as capable, and just as much a part of me as Jesus, Buddha, or any of the masters. Believe in your abilities. Then you must learn to be patient. Some creations take longer than others. Change will become apparent when your creation has been completed.

God, I know that one of the keys to healing the body is to learn to love it regardless of its shape and condition. Please teach us how to really love our bodies especially when they are not in the condition that we would prefer.

Okay. When you stop thinking of yourself as defective you will learn to love your body. For example, many of you are weight conscious. Why would having extra fat make you feel defective?

I guess we bought into society's perception that thin equates to beauty. More importantly, for most of us, having extra fat is a health issue.

You are a good example. You've stopped thinking of yourself as beautiful since you've gained some weight, but that is not beauty. I am going to tell you what real beauty is. Beauty is every time you do something kind for another. Beauty is every time you bless another. Beauty is every positive thought you have, every time you give of yourself to help another, every loving word, and beauty is what you are. You are so very beautiful. My beautiful teacher feels unattractive because she may not be as thin or as young as she used to be. Know that no matter what the youth and advertising companies say you will still be the beautiful spirit I chose as my messenger and master teacher. You love with your being and that is beautiful. I wish you would be open to the beauty that is you—your spirit. Now how could you love the body?

Please teach me so that I may help others who feel as frustrated as I.

We have been working on showing you the many layers of a person. Your physical body is the dense part of your total being. What is true is that the soul houses the body—not the body housing the soul. The body is merely what is reflected in the mirror. It is the layers around your body that reflect the beauty of your spirit. You look like a diamond with brilliant white reflecting all the shimmering iridescent colors around you. You shine. You sparkle. You glisten. You reflect who you are and what we see is beautiful. How you wish to see spirit is how they see you.

How can we learn to love that image while looking into the physical being in the mirror?

Dear, you all need to look beyond the mirror.

How can we learn not to care about what we see and experience with our five senses?

Dear Ones, will you trust me?

Yes.

Okay. I am going to tell you to close your eyes and to picture yourself as thin and healthy. Find pictures of yourself as you looked at the weight you were when you were happy with your body. For those people who have never experienced happiness with how they have looked, find pictures in a magazine and cut out those pictures of how you would like to look. Choose pictures of people that are at an appropriate weight for your body frame. Not everyone is healthy in a size two, four, or even a ten. For some that are tall or have a larger bone structure maybe a size sixteen is more realistic. Put the pictures up around the house. Forget the scale for three weeks. Be strong enough to believe in spite of physical evidence.

So you're saying that visualization is enough for any of us to change things?

No, that is not enough.

Step 1 is visualization.

Step 2 is *frequent* positive self-talks. Once or twice a day is not enough. Keep repeating to your subconscious how you are programming yourself to be. Say it every time you remember it. Say it aloud and with conviction.

Step 3 is to have faith in your abilities. You *can* heal yourself. All of you can. Keep telling yourself about what I see. All of you are worth the effort. You are worth the belief. You are worth every wonderful thought and every beautiful vision you can have. See your total being not just your body. When you visualize yourself visualize your spirit shining around the body. I have faith that all of you who wish to make changes in your life have the ability to do so. Now have faith in yourselves.

People need to find a way to see beyond the mirror. I have found a way for myself that I am happy to share. One night when I was feeling miserable about myself I meditated to see who inside of me (an inner child or an inner adult) was so upset. I invited my "higher self", that is my spirit, to join me in my meditation. At one point, she asked me to look at her and to describe what I saw. As I looked at her she began changing form from a physical person into a person made of brilliant white-golden light and beautiful colors that sparkled like a diamond in sunlight. She then moved into me and became part of me. She produced a full-length mirror and asked me to look into the mirror and to describe myself. Instead of seeing a physical body I now saw myself as a beautiful sparkling brilliant white-gold light body. Now when I look into the mirror I can look past the mirror image and see that beautiful light body. This must be what you mean when you say to look beyond the mirror.

Thank you for sharing that.

Let's continue speaking about frustration. It's really all a question of attitude. Everyone experiences some level of frustration at some time. The question is: how will you deal with it and how long will you allow the frustration to interrupt your life? Are you holding on to it to draw attention to yourself? Are you using it as an excuse to keep from moving forward? Are you letting your fears hide behind frustration? That's a big reason. A goodly portion of frustration is resistance to facing your fears and to making changes.

Let me explain to you how things work. As you have heard many times before, what you resist persists. The harder you resist the longer your challenges will hold on. As this book is going through your filters I know that you (and millions of others) are concerned with weight so let's use that as our example. Monitoring your food intake preoccupies much of your thought. It is like you are fighting with yourself so much of the time. You have a tendency to fall into the old pattern of eating what you like then chastising yourself afterward. Each night you go to bed thinking that the next day you will have a fresh start and that you can release the weight.

You do your self-talks and tell yourself that you are getting thinner and healthier every moment, but you still do not have the faith that these talks are really working. You even talk yourself out of it by saying how frustrated you are that the body is comfortable at this weight and won't change. Don't think that you are alone in doing this. Why do you think that so many people have a weight challenge? They are doing exactly the same things you do.

How do you get off of the merry-go-round?

<u>First</u>, stop *all* of the negative talk even if it is to be funny. I know that one of the ways that you deal with painful situations is with humor. If you must say jokes turn them around into a positive statement.

<u>Second</u>, just *be* with your body. Accept it as it is and learn to love it exactly as it is. You gained the weight for very good reasons, and it has served you well by fulfilling those reasons. When you have released those reasons because they no longer serve you then the weight will come off. Intellectually you wish to lose weight because you know that it affects your health. Emotionally, however, you are still holding onto your fears, your anger, or whatever is triggering your reason for keeping the weight. Many of you still equate food with love. When you are sure that you no longer need those emotional reasons process out the fear, the anger, the sadness, or whatever you feel. If you can't release it by yourself then get help.

<u>Third</u>, visualize your body as you would like it to look, but stop beating yourself up about it if it doesn't look like that. It may not begin to physically show immediately. If you make a food choice that is not as healthy for you it's okay. Just keep going from there. Every moment is a new moment and a new start. The irony is that when you finally learn to love yourself just as you are and stop criticizing the mirror image then that is when the weight will come off.

Loving your self and accepting yourself for who you are does not mean giving up. See yourself as thin and healthy. Tell yourself frequently that you are thin and healthy. The self-talks are for the purpose of implanting those thoughts upon your subconscious mind.

<u>Fourth</u>, be who you wish to be. You have a wonderful example in Mary Kay Ash with whom you have been associated for many years. She frequently said, "Fake it 'till you make it." *Be* thin and healthy in your mind and attitude. In other words, if you were a thin and healthy

person what would you wish to be eating? This will probably require you to change some of your eating habits. How much would you enjoy exercising? Would a thin and healthy person be content or happy with herself? (The answer to that one is probably "not necessarily", but if that has been your main concern then your answer may be, "yes." Then let it go.) Trust that you are indeed making changes.

Many times if you still see no visual changes you become angry and frustrated. Do you not know that by returning to those emotions you are re-creating the condition? What you must remember is that sometimes there are immediate visible results, but sometimes there is a time delay. Your emotional and mental work has affected the quality of the new cells that form in your body on a constant basis. When new cells come into your body they are healthy and perfect. After a time, however, they begin to take on the qualities or diseases of existing cells. When you are trying to improve a condition, program the new cells to retain their health and energy. Let the new cells multiply the health and welfare of your body. Remember, though, that new cells don't replace old cells all at once. It takes a bit of time for old cells to die so you have a time delay with many conditions. You cannot always expect to go to sleep sick or diseased and awaken completely healthy. It depends on your condition. It's like losing weight. You can't expect to go to sleep and to awaken fifty pounds lighter. (I also would like you to remember that I am speaking to the general populace. The masters can make immediate changes. They have allowed themselves to *know* the oneness with God and all of God's creations. When you reach this level of mastery what you call "miraculous changes" can occur.)

Many of you have reached a high level of belief in your abilities to heal yourselves, but you have not reached that last little bit that brings you to the faith of knowing without any question of doubt. When after a period of time you still do not see the results that you desire, you let your doubts and fears overtake your faith. You do not see the inner workings of the cells bringing you closer and closer to a state of compete healing. Don't give up!

Attitude combats frustration. Keep a positive attitude that you are changing your body every minute of every day. Remember that the new little cells that are being born within your body continually are completely healthy and are helping you to create a healthy body. Don't contaminate them with negativity and doubt. Visualize these fit and healthy cells growing in your body and taking over the unhealthy cells and the fat cells. Before you know it you will begin seeing physical changes. You will begin feeling more energetic and healthy. You will begin awakening with new strength and conviction in your abilities.

There are thousands of you that have kept that faith and completed what doctors have called "miracles." Look at all of those people that have "somehow" cured their cancer or made tumors disappear. Look at the people that were told that they would never walk again and yet are walking. Look at the people who have been physically confined to wheelchairs but continue to lead fairly normal and productive lives. There are countless stories of self-healing and encouragement for you to read.

Those of you who have chosen to use your healing abilities to help others know that if the patient will allow healing to take place it will—even if it is not apparent to the eye. However, you seem to have a more difficult time allowing yourself to accept that same universal healing. Have patience. Have trust. If you have difficulty trusting yourself, trust God. You are the body of God. Do not your scriptures tell you that you are made in the image of God? What that means is that you were created from that energy and power. You are part of that energy in its purest form.

You are never too old to start making whatever changes are beneficial *right now*. Stop living in the past. Stop living in the future. The *only* time that is important is *now*—this moment. Enjoy and celebrate each moment. I know that there are times when you feel either physical or emotional pain. I know that there are times when you feel that you are living in a nightmare. Try to remember that there are no accidents; everything is happening for a very good reason. Try to find the blessing of every situation. Try to find the blessing of every condition. Everything depends upon one's perspective. Try to learn why something is happening to you (actually, from you). What are you to learn from this experience? Stop blaming anyone else for where you find yourself. You are responsible for your life. Face up to it without self-derision or guilt. Deal with it. Roll up your sleeves and push through your frustration and fears.

As Mary Kay Ash said, "When you reach the end of your rope, tie a knot and hold on."

That's it. Remember that you are not alone—ever. If your hands should slip, we will catch you if you fall.

All of you feel frustrated at some time. Not everyone is concerned with his body. Many people feel frustrated in the area of relationships. We hear you complain that you keep attracting the same kind of person to you over and over or that you cannot find anyone with whom to have a relationship. Once again, what you resist persists. You will keep attracting to you the same type of person until you say, "I have had enough." What is it that these people have in common? Why do you keep drawing them to you? What is the "lesson" that you need to learn? When you have figured this out, when you have had your experience (learned your lesson), then the people in your life who no longer serve you will begin leaving your life.

Sometimes, to end a relationship may be very painful. Know that it is important to release it so that you can begin attracting people with different qualities. Your soul will lead you to where you will meet a new type of person.

Perhaps it is in your plan to learn to be independent or to learn to be content being physically alone with yourself. It may be your soul's yearning for you to learn to listen to the silence, to experience that still small voice within, and to find that spark of God. Your experience may be that of learning to trust your own judgment and to find your inner strength.

Each person has his own agenda. You have the responsibility of figuring out why you are in the situation or condition in which you find yourself. If you are not satisfied with where you are you have the responsibility to make changes in your life. If you are completely satisfied, fulfilled, and happy with every area of your life, please go out and help others. We could use the assistance.

Sometimes frustrations are an outgrowth of boredom. If there is no sense of purpose or direction a person can easily reach a level of frustration. More often than not, people meander through life unless they have been given direction by their parents or have a strong ambition. People often move from job to job or house to house while always complaining. Do you not realize that happiness comes from within? When you are happy with yourself and when you know that you are truly one with everything, you shall feel peace and contentment. The location of a home, the job you do, or your relationships with others will always be comfortable when you have learned self-love. It doesn't matter if you prefer a life of solitude or a life of bustling activity. Contentment can be found within each.

"So," you ask, "how does one reach this inner contentment?" It is reached by truly knowing yourself and recognizing your self-worth. Here is an exercise for you:

1. Every night before you go to sleep take five or more minutes to reflect on your day.

2. Each day list three or more loving things that you have done. It can be either for your self or for someone else. These can be small acts of kindness such as holding a door for someone whose hands were full, saying an encouraging or kind thing to someone, meditating, taking time for self improvement, reading something spiritual, or saying your daily affirmations.

3. Each day list three or more positive attributes that you demonstrated. Were you being loving, kind, thoughtful, considerate, honest, or trustworthy?

Do these exercises every day and you will notice changes happening. Confidence will build. You will really start liking who you are. If you see negative attributes sneaking into that list, cancel them and work on changing them into positive attributes. Have you been judgmental? Did you tell lies? Did you disappoint someone? Did you disappoint yourself? What can you do to change that behavior?

Self-analyzation brings self-clarity. It's important to know who you are. If you are not how you would like to be—change. You can do it. You are in charge of your attitude. You are in charge of the words you speak to others and to yourself. You are in charge of your actions.

We have also noticed that your frustrations are accumulative. You are permitting the tiny daily frustrations to compound until they begin to feel over-whelming. So, as you can guess, if you handle each little incident at the time of its occurrence then you won't have the major frustrations that accrue. I know that this is simplistic, but it is the easiest answer. I also know that it can become more complicated.

Say, for instance, that there is a health situation that you are trying to correct. You keep trying to ascertain the origin of the creation. You are following our suggestions. Still the condition appears to remain imbedded in your body. We understand how frustration builds over a period of time. Please, don't give up. Keep doing the work required. Clear the conditions, process out the anger or pain, visualize yourself as well and healthy, and truly forgive yourself and learn to love yourself and your body just as you are.

The speaker changed at this point.

I would like to continue the discussion on how to handle frustrations at the time of their occurrences. I know that it is easy to discuss intellectually being frustrated. I also know that it is a whole different matter when it is your emotions that have dominated the situation.

When you have reached the level of frustration that has sent you into an emotional tailspin you cry out for relief and help.

Intellectually you know that punching something, crying, or whining, will not solve your dilemma. It appeases your emotions, however, to do these things. Have your "pity-party" if it makes you feel better. However, put a limit on the time you allot. Allow yourself to be miserable for a short while. Don't inflict yourself on other people when you are in this state. You are doing a disservice to another by sharing your negativity. Are you doing a disservice to yourself by allowing yourself to be temporarily miserable? No, of course you are not. In fact, you are being kind to yourself. By permitting yourself this indulgence you are releasing the pain and negativity. Let yourself cry; it releases toxins. Let yourself punch a punching bag or pillow; it releases the anger or frustration. I always liked your making bread to release your anger. Every time you punched down the dough it released a little more. By the time you finished you always felt better and loving and then could enjoy a delicious loaf of bread with your family.

I didn't realize that anyone was watching.

I am always watching all of you. I always know everything you do, say, think, or feel. How can I not when you are part of me? Stop worrying that you will be judged. I encourage you to choose activities that will hasten your spiritual progression, but I gave you free will and I will not interfere with your choices. Nor will I punish you for whatever you choose. I love you no matter what. It is important for you to experience the negative as well as the positive.

I would like to close this chapter with a little story. Once upon a time there was a little spirit that enjoyed flitting around heaven. He loved spending his days playing on fluffy clouds, listening to the beautiful music of the heavenly angels' choir, and visiting with his loving friends. He spent many centuries like this enjoying the sunshine and perfect weather during the days and counting the twinkling stars at night.

After a while, though, he started to feel that there must be more to life than this. He began to ask his friends if they had seen other places or things. They told him stories of hatred and wars. They told him about the behavior of people who lied, stole, inflicted great pain, and murdered.

Well, as you might suspect, the little spirit began to have nightmares after listening to these terrible stories. Having lived all of his life in the perfection of a loving environment he questioned the validity of these tales. So he went to the Creator to ascertain if they were true. He was told that yes, they were actual things that were happening on the earth. At that, the little spirit was more puzzled than ever before. If things were so terrible there why would anyone choose to go to earth? The Creator explained to the little spirit that it was a great blessing to experience these things because only by seeing the negative things could one truly know and appreciate all of the wonderful things.

The little spirit thought about that for a while and knew that the Creator was right. He had always taken for granted his peaceful existence. Yet in his heart he knew that there had to be more. It was not so much that he was bored, but that he felt no sense of purpose.

The little spirit went back to the Creator with determination. He would go to earth to help people to act lovingly and kind to each other. Of course, he wouldn't eliminate all negativity because, after all, everyone needed some negativity for comparison. He was determined to make a difference.

So he was sent down to earth as he wished. However, a funny thing happened. As he descended to earth to be born his memories began to be erased. He forgot why he had chosen to go to earth. So until well into his adulthood he toiled, he failed in his relationships and his work efforts, he found himself physically ill with many aches and pains, and he grew angry and frustrated as the years progressed.

However, one day, he saw a light in the darkness. He began to awaken from his spiritual slumber. He read books that told him that he could change his life by adjusting his attitude. He listened to speakers that encouraged him to assume responsibility for his actions and to take charge of his life. He began to meditate and to look within for answers to his deepest questions.

Slowly he began to remember why he had chosen to go to the earth. He continued his journey with a renewed sense of purpose. Eventually he became a messenger and encouraged others to heal their pain. He taught others to trust in God and in their own abilities and to learn to love themselves as well as others.

Finally the day came for him to return to heaven. Excitedly he greeted his friends and told them about the wonderful experiences he had had while on earth. Instead of being excited, however, his friends looked at him quizzically. Hadn't he seen any hatred and war? Hadn't he met any liars, cheaters, or murderers? "Yes," he replied, "but now I understand why people act as they do. I've seen both sides of human behavior. I learned that only by experiencing one can you truly understand the other. I also understand that we can change our attitudes and behaviors if we desire to do so. No matter how hurt, how angry, or how frustrated we feel, we can survive those feelings. We can change our situations. We can heal our lives. We can take what appears to be a terrible situation and find what good can come out of it. We are truly powerful beings with the ability to do anything that we set our minds and hearts to do. Even though, at the time, some of the experiences I had were very negative and hurtful, I can look back and feel grateful for having had them because of all that I have learned."

Thank you, God, for that encouraging story. Sometimes we get so involved in a situation that it's hard to see the forest for the trees. Thank you for reminding us that everything is a matter of perspective. The next time that I feel frustrated or angry I will try to remember what you've told us.

You'll probably forget during your "pity party," but I know that eventually it will resurface and my little messenger will continue to spread the light. I encourage you (all of you) to remember that even in your darkest moments you are never alone. Dear, as your mother used to say, "This, too, shall pass." When things are at their bleakest, just hold on. The next moment you may turn a corner and find a miracle.

8

Fighting Anxiety

At this juncture in time you have requested that we include a chapter that deals with anxiety. Since the events of September 11, 2001, there are many who have been experiencing what they call "attacks of anxiety." What these so-called "attacks" are based on is the direct result of one of the great illusions that society has accepted as reality. That is the illusion that one is actually able to die. I tell you this: life is eternal. You cannot die. You can only change form. When you accept this as the true reality those "attacks" will stop.

God, some people are not afraid of dying; they are afraid of not living. They have young children about whom they worry and don't wish to leave. They have things that they would still like to accomplish.

This is true, but let's put it all into a different perspective. Every soul that chooses to incarnate is a complete soul that has been in existence for millennia. It is born into a little body that, in the beginning, does require much physical and emotional care. Let's remember, though, that every soul comes equipped with an agenda. It is entirely possible that when he was planning the circumstances that would afford him the most opportunity to "learn his lessons" he may have selected to come into a situation whereby one or both of his parents would be eliminated early on in his life.

I realize that everyone has free will and that he or she has the opportunity to make changes. However, the broad agenda of each person is generally programmed in advance. When you are home, in this dimension, heaven, or whatever you call "here," it is possible to see a prediction of what you call "the future."

Time is perceived differently here. You see time as a linear projection. It is a difficult concept to understand for most of you, but time is not linear. It is more like a vertical fold or a circle. In other words, the past, present, and future are actually happening simultaneously and can impact each other. Events can be seen here before you perceive them. That is how you are able to choose your circumstances. It's natural that a parent would consciously wish to remain with his or her child. When faced with danger he may think about all of the adventures and experiences with the child that he would be missing.

Let's remember, though, that the parent also has a planned agenda. His spirit may have been one to volunteer to give his life in the attacks of September 11, 2001. Yes, you heard me correctly. Before they incarnated, those loving souls volunteered to die that day as a gesture that would bring together people and nations for peace. The conscious mind had forgotten that, but the spirit made sure that they were where they were supposed to be. If that was not in their program they got out of the twin towers alive.

You are letting the fear that you can actually die intensify until your every movement and thought becomes an exercise in fear. You are letting your imaginations grow. If you do not change your thinking, that is what will become your reality. Yes, your thoughts will actually create your reality. Is this how you wish to live the rest of this lifetime? Are you afraid to fly in an airplane because there may be a terrorist on board? Are you afraid to take any form of transportation because there may be a bomb attached? Are you afraid to cross the street because a car might hit you? Are you afraid to go into a public building or attend a public function because you might be attacked? Are you even afraid to breathe because you might catch anthrax? Is this how you wish to spend your days? I am not suggesting that you become oblivious to your surroundings or careless, but I am suggesting that you re-think your attitude.

Of course, the choice is yours. Let's make this clearer. What is the worst thing that could happen to you? It is the illusion that you can die. Your body *is* going to die. So the question is: how will it die? Are you afraid that it will die before you have reached a mature age? What would happen if you were in a car "accident?" How about creating a fatal disease like cancer or aids? Or, maybe you would prefer loading up your body with cholesterol and having a heart attack. Why not kill yourself with an overdose of drugs or alcohol? Or perhaps, you would prefer to get emphysema from smoking. Are you any less afraid to die slowly as a result of your choices than quickly in an explosion?

What will happen once your body dies? You will come "home." Your friends and loved ones that are here in spirit will greet you. You will remember everything that you had forgotten when you left to experience this lifetime. You will once again feel the unconditional love that is ever present. You will know once again that all are one and all are God.

Why do you choose to wait until that time to know that, in truth, you are already part of the whole? You are already eternal. You do not have to live this life in fear.

People tell me that the feelings of anxiety quickly overcome them and that they feel helpless. Just taking a breath or meditating doesn't seem to help. What aid can we give to those people that will help them to release the fears?

I see that we will have to address this further. You can control your thinking. I know that thoughts come unbidden into your mind. When this happens you do have the control to change those thoughts. If you start to feel anxious ask yourself what it is that you fear. Is it pain? Is it separation from your loved ones? Is it going to the unknown? Is it regret? What will happen to you if you leave? You will survive and your family will survive, for in truth, how can you not? You may survive here and they may survive there, but survive you all will.

Instead of worrying about what might happen to you why do you not live every day as if it were to be your last day on earth? Tell your loved ones and friends that you love and appreciate them. Hug and kiss your children. Help a stranger with an act of kindness. Marvel at a beautiful sunrise or sunset. Plant some flowers. Really listen to music. Let your eyes feast on a painting. Write a note of encouragement or thanks.

Become the master that you are innately. Change the illusion that you are a separate being. You are part of the whole of everything that I have created. You are part of every other person no matter what their color or philosophy. I love *all* of you—every single one of my creations. You may not agree with the philosophy of your neighbor. In reality, however, there is no right or wrong; it is all a matter of perspective.

You are part of everything in nature, every molecule, and every atom in the universe. Once you know that, once you accept that each and every one of you is a part of the whole, your life will change. When you truly "realize" or "make real" this truth there will be no more wars, no more murder, no more rape or abuse, no more hunger, no more poverty, and no more superiority. You will know that by being one hurting another is hurting yourself. Causing another to be hungry or unloved is bringing that upon your self.

I am a bit confused about that last sentence. How can not contributing to a charity that donates food to a third world country affect what you have on your table, for example?

Causing another hunger is only a metaphor. It's a hunger for knowledge, a hunger for love, a hunger for wisdom, or a hunger for help. What you give out will come back to you ten fold.

You're talking about purposefully withholding help or helpful information.

Yes.

As a teacher, I would challenge that statement. It is our job as teachers to help people to think for themselves. If we continually give the answers how will they learn to think?

Now you're thinking. You are correct from that perspective. From another side, why hold back progress by having people repeat steps? By sharing information progress moves faster and farther.

That's also true. To return to the original statement, though, how will it be brought back ten fold?

Okay. I see that I will have to elaborate. It's like throwing a pebble into the water. Every thought and every deed has a ripple effect into the universe. If you withhold love or if you withhold help the associated thoughts still ripple out. My question is: are you sending out positive or negative ripples into the universe? Those ripples will bounce back to you every time they come up against another thought or deed. Thoughts, when they strike similar thoughts, stick together. Then more thoughts stick to these until you have one massive thought.

That is how the collective consciousness works, isn't it?

That's excellent. Yes, the collective consciousness has the power to affect every individual in its path. It can affect religions, diseases, politics, time, and even weather. So, as it bounces back, will the sender not be affected on many levels?

Yes, I can see where we would be hit with it either on a positive or a negative level.

Good. Many of you are still asking, "How could God have let such atrocities happen?" You still do not take responsibility for your own actions. You create the environment for such events to take place by your collective thoughts. The so called "atrocities" will stop when you learn to tolerate opinions that differ from your own, when you learn to share all the resources, and when you learn to live amicably with people of different races and beliefs. As long as those in power refuse to share the wealth, the resources, or the basic necessities things will continue as they are. You don't even afford basic living conditions to most of the world. If everyone were entitled to habitation, sustenance, and medical care, there would not be thousands dying every day because of the greed of power hungry political leaders. Your collective consciousness has brought you to the present state. The fear that is manifested within these conditions is anxiety.

What is anxiety? The dictionary defines it as a worry or uneasiness about what may happen. The key word here is "may." You like to deal in numbers. Okay. The odds are fairly astronomical against that you will be in an airplane that will fly into a building or that you will be in a building that will be hit by an airplane. If it is in your master plan to be in that building then that is where you are meant to be. If your soul has agreed that you are to be a "hero or victim" to help bring the nations of the world around to peace and accord, then that is where you will be. If it is not in your agenda to be there then you will not be there. Your conscious mind may not know your agenda but your spirit does. You will always be where you should be at the time you should be there for a very good reason. There is always a purpose. There are no accidents. There are no coincidences. So to what purpose is worrying? Have you not noticed that ninety-eight percent of your worrying never comes to fruition?

I would like to pass along a suggestion if I may.

Please do. It's a good one.

I attended a lecture years ago where the speaker told of something she did that was helpful. She decorated a shoe-box and cut a slit in the top. This became her "worry box." Every time she began to worry about something she would write it on a slip of paper and put it into the box. Then she would forget about it. She designated two hours every Thursday afternoon to worry about everything that was in the box. Surprisingly, however, when she began to sift through the papers, she found that about ninety-eight per-cent of her worries never materialized. She only had to deal with the last two percent.

Worry is needless. If it persists you will only create dis-ease within your physical body. The next time the anxiety sneaks into your emotions use your mind and logic to release it. You can overcome your emotions. Find the fear. If you cannot logically release it, visualize it. Give it a shape, a color, a feeling, a sound, or a taste in your body. Find a way to release that expression. Do it in meditation or hypnosis. Tears or laughter can be a form of release. If you need a physical release punch a pillow or a punching bag. Do a physical activity with all of your strength. As you do these things tell yourself that you are releasing your fears and your worries. Let your body, your mind, and your spirit work together to keep you healthy.

I know that this will be difficult for many of you to accept, but I permit all happenings. I created everything. Do you not think that I could stop anything from happening if that is what I wished? Does it not follow that I wish to permit all that you cause with the free will that I have given you? If I stopped your actions would I not be taking away your free will? I wish to experience everything, and that I do through you my beloved children.

I'm going to tell you a little story. Once upon a time there lived a little angel. He lived alone in a far away place just on the edge of the universe. For many eons he felt content to wander the hills enjoying the soft breezes and verdant plants and flowers. He reveled in the exquisite natural creations around him. His music was the gurgling of the streams and the crashing waves of the oceans upon the shores. His art was the tapestry of the stars at night and the wondrous painting of the sky at dawn and dusk. He marveled at the changing colors of the leaves in the autumn and at the flowering trees in the spring. In the winter he played in the soft fresh snow and contemplated the uniqueness of each snowflake. This he did season after season and century after century.

Until this point he had been quite content singing to himself and talking to the unseen Creator. One day, while enjoying the sweet aroma of the flowers, he startled himself with the thought that it might be nice to share this paradise with another angel. So that evening before going to bed, he asked The Creator for someone with whom he could share this bountiful beauty.

The next morning when he awoke he eagerly rushed out of his home to see if his wish had been granted. He was determined to search far and wide for his companion. Until now, The Creator had met his every need. Therefore, he expected that he would now have a friend. His journey took him across oceans, through deserts and forests, and over mountains.

Finally, from the top of a hill, he espied in the distance an intriguing sight. He saw many buildings of various heights clustered together. He heard the strange sounds of horns, whistles, and machinery. As he walked closer to the city he noticed the changes that were becoming apparent in his beautiful paradise. He saw trash littered along the path. He smelled a pungent aroma coming from the river that flowed a short distance away. When he peered into the water to investigate he noticed that it was muddy instead of the clear fresh water to which he had become accustomed. There were no fish swimming around.

He felt puzzled and became increasingly uneasy as he continued toward the city. He soon found himself beginning to cough because the polluted air over the city began to impede his breathing. He thought, hopefully, that if he could find the companion he requested, then all of this would be worth the effort.

Finally, he entered the city and was stunned by what he saw. Instead of one companion there were thousands of people. The noise was cacophonous. He couldn't believe his eyes and his ears. The people were yelling and arguing with each other. They were fighting and killing each other. He couldn't understand what was happening. He cried out to The Creator in puzzlement for an explanation.

Quietly, The Creator answered him. "In the beginning, there was only me. I am all that was, all that is, and all that will be. I could not, however, see my magnificence without seeing what was not magnificent. How can one see greatness, if greatness is all that there is? So in order to know my immenseness I created the opportunity to know what was not immense. I took portions of myself and created beings that were different parts of my energy. I endowed each being with unique attributes. All the beings were part of me and all the attributes are mine. I wished to experience all that could be experienced by these beings so that I could fully experience myself. I gave to each the free will to create his own experiences and to make his own choices. This gave me the unlimited range to experience everything. So for me, there is nothing that is bad or ugly. I relish all experiences because from my perspective they are all positive.

At first all of my children were blissful and loving. They remembered that they were all part of the whole. However, as time went on they forgot this and focused on their individual differences. Thus they began to create illusions and stories to substantiate these illusions. The more they believed these stories the more they became real. Thus, they were creating new realities. They forgot that these realities were built on illusions and, therefore, were illusions in themselves.

Even their perception of me began to change. I became a creator who was vengeful, demanding, and judgmental. They thought that if their behavior was not as they perceived that I would wish, then, of course, I would punish them with eternal damnation. This is pure rubbish. It assumes that I would need anything from them. I don't need anything. I love them. Why would I ever punish any of them for giving me the experiences for which I created them?

The more these illusions became real the more illusions they created to fix the prior illusions. Their feelings of separateness from me and from each other lead to feelings of superiority and inferiority. These lead to selfishness, greed, power, envy, and myriad of other emotions. Ultimately, this resulted in what you see before you. You see anger, hurt, murder, rape, abuse, war, and violence. You also see its opposite: love, caring, healing, nurturing, and friendship. Remember that one will balance out the other so that we may experience everything.

Little angel, do not feel forlorn. Know that there is a purpose for what you see before you. Hurting the environment of your beautiful paradise leads to healing what I have created. By creating loss is appreciation born.

My children will see that hurting each other will lead to awakening the memories of our oneness. Calamity brings people of all differences together. So don't fret. Eventually people will realize that they must work together for their own benefit. They will realize that to harm the environment is to their own detriment.

Whether you stay and help them to awaken their memories of what is real or leave them to their own devices is your choice. I will not try to influence you. I will love you as I love every one of them regardless of your choices."

The little angel sat for a long time and thought about everything that The Creator had said. He thought about the beauty and serenity of his home. He thought about his loneliness. He thought about the effort that it would take to help the people of the city and the conditions that they had created. He knew that he would face criticism, skepticism, fear, and anger, and would have to work hard to awaken the people to the truth. He also knew that it was what he wished to do. So he rolled up his sleeves and went forth to talk to the people.

My children, there are many messengers and masters walking among you at this time. They all carry the same messages: We are one. What hurts one hurts another. Do unto others what you would have them do unto you. There is no superiority. There is enough of everything. Love is unconditional and unlimited.

PART II
Healing Your Body

9

Am I Putting My Best Foot Forward?

Let's begin on the ground floor, so to speak, with the feet. This chapter is not concerned with the slight injury of stubbing your toe because you were not paying attention to where you were walking. It is addressing the many people that have constant foot pains and problems. Feet must be given a whole chapter in the book because they are reflective of so many things. Generally, however, though they may feel very painful pains in the foot are indicative of minor concerns unless they are related to other parts of the body. For example, if the foot problems are a side effect of diabetes the issues with which to deal are those of that disease rather than the foot.

Each toe and each part of the foot indicates something different.

I have a general question. What is reflexology that equates each part of the foot with another part of the body?

Reflexology of the foot is a method of noting where there are correlating areas of the body that require attention. We will include mention of these areas when it is appropriate.

Do the fingers and toes have corresponding issues?

Some digits concern the same issues.

<u>The Little Toe</u>

Let's begin with the little toe. The little toe suggests how you deal with "lessons" of will. In the overall scope of breaks this is a minor issue. When the little toe is broken the person has been "broken" of his free will and should look to whom he has given control. When someone acquiesces to another's will sometimes it's for a valid compromise. This is fine except when the person feels he is being forced against his will and resents it. Yes, there are times when this happens. Yes, there are times that control will be in someone else's hands, but the issue is, how you deal with it. If you do not choose to either accept it, learn to live with it, or take back your will, chances are that it will show up in the little toe.

The underlying remedy is: if the control is out of your hands you must keep a positive outlook. This has happened to you because your soul wished this as an experience. If you voluntarily have given up control either you wished to experience strengthening of will and have chosen this as a method of regaining your assertiveness, or have given your will as a gift to the other for their benefit. Look to see why you have given away your free will. Either give it with love or take it back. This could be a lesson of communication.

The Fourth Toe

The fourth toe injuries indicate love lessons with regard to unity or lack of unity. When this toe is sore it shows that you need to deal with the generally minor irritations in relationships. Deal with each annoyance immediately instead of letting it compound with others until they grow into a major confrontation. Speak gently and lovingly. Don't verbally attack or criticize the other person. Instead, comment on the irritation. For example, don't say, "You're a dummy." Instead, say, "For a smart person, that was not a very smart thing that you did." Communicate. Write a letter. Call on the phone. What is happening here is that those little irritations are being stored in this toe.

The Center Toe

The center toe will indicate both getting and giving of joy. When you have made a soul decision to block joy from your life it will show on this toe. Repeated clumsiness and stubbing your toe should cause you to look at the reasons for lacking joy. Are you looking for attention? Are you playing the "poor me" game? Are you letting your anger block a love of anything? What would it take for you to release this blockage? How would it change your life? Are you willing to change your life?

The Second Toe

The second toe deals with issues of a temporary emotional hurt. Keep in mind that the initial hurt is minor. Don't hold it inside of you while you let it fester for days, weeks, months, or even years. That is how a minor hurt builds until it can become a major ailment. So many times the one who has said the things that have triggered your pain does not even know that you have allowed yourself to feel hurt. Most people are not mind readers; they don't know unless you tell them.

There is something else to consider. What is your pay back for holding on to that hurt? Are you looking for sympathy? Do you wish to play the victim? The more you think about it the larger you create it. Wouldn't it be more healing to let it go? Can't you tell that person that you feel hurt by what was said? He or she probably never intended to hurt you and would prefer to help mend your relationship. If you don't let that person know what hurts you, what is to stop them from repeating the hurt? Do you trust that person enough to be honest with your feelings? If you can't be honest, what are you getting out of that relationship? Love is being honest with your self and with that other person.

Make a list of what is beneficial to you and the other person if you give up the pain and compromise or let go all together. How will it change your lives for the better? Looking for positive changes takes some of what you call "soul searching."

It is probable that the issues are not with another but would require change within yourself. Look at what inner changes would enrich your life. I'm talking to each person. Let go. Trust yourself to make the changes that will help your spiritual growth.

If you feel that you cannot confront the person that hurt you, write out your feelings. Then destroy the letter. Clearing out the emotional pain will keep you healthy. Vengeance serves no healthy purpose. Replaying the hurt over and over in your mind serves no healthy purpose. Love yourself enough to let it go.

The four toes of which we have been speaking correspond to the sinuses. You will notice that the concerns of these toes and the concerns of the sinus area are directly related. Both of these areas are indications that there are relationship irritations and control issues.

The Large Toe

The large toe concerns the biggest issues within the toe area. When the big toe is painful, this indicates stubbornness.

In reflexology, isn't pain in this toe corresponding to the neck?

It does correspond to some extent. Stubbornness has been called "stiff necked," so in that respect, yes, but it's more that the toe is holding on to this stubbornness with a tight grip.

It's pride, too. Look to see why you are being so tenacious. Is it the issue itself or your reluctance to admit an error? What principle is so important that wishing is painful to you? You must decide whether holding on to your issues will enhance your experience or delay it. Look inward to your stubbornness. You can release it by writing in a journal or meditating. Go on and try letting go. Sometimes it takes great love to let go of issues you've been embracing.

Toe Fungus

What about toe fungus or athlete's foot?

Let's look at fungus on the toes. Situations that arise in childhood and are suppressed for a long time can manifest themselves by becoming embedded in the toenails. This is why toe fungus is prevalent over a number of years. Events that occur as early as birth can be imbedded and manifest as fungus—a growth, so to speak, of deeply forgotten issues. The remedy is to remember and to deal with those childhood issues. Medications can physically clear away the fungus, but if you do not clear away the initial cause it can manifest elsewhere in the body.

Can this be past life issues?

They are not usually from a past life in this area.

Cramping or Arthritis

What about those people with arthritis or cramping?

These are two different things. Cramping is a temporary indication that you must let go of stress and tension. Physically stretch out the muscles. Mentally relax the muscles. See what is causing stress. Slow down a bit if you have been putting physical stress on the muscles.

Could cramping just be the result of a lack of a vitamin or mineral?

That could be the physical catalyst, but look, too, for the underlying cause.

Arthritis says something different. It indicates your rigidity. It's telling you to re-evaluate your views. Why are you being rigid and stiff? Arthritis is a subconscious means of preventing you from walking forward. What is the fear that has you held so stiffly in place? Are you afraid to make changes in your life? Are you allowing criticism from others to be the basis of how you think about yourself? Are you letting resentment keep you from advancing? Yes, there is medication and there are physical remedies that will help ease the discomfort, but they are only topical fixes. When you release the underlying fears you will truly heal yourself. You must believe. Trust in yourself. You have the ability to heal yourself. Whether you choose to is up to you.

The Heel

Let's continue with the bottom of the foot. Those who have heel spurs or have your soreness at the heel have a tendency to make yourselves stiff. You call it "digging in your heels" or stubbornness. It's a reflection of how you handle your life at home. With soreness you have a tendency to have things your way. Let go of stiffness. Let go of control issues. When spurs occur it's an indication that this has been your pattern for a long time. Yes, maybe even past lives are being carried into this life. Your attitude may need a re-evaluation.

The Plantar

If the plantar or arch is sore you let so much get to your emotional body. How sensitive the person is who is sore in this area. The healing is to let your self be compassionate but not to take everything into yourself emotionally. It's fine to be sensitive, but it doesn't have to become part of your astral body.

This area of the foot corresponds with the colon and intestines in that the issues relate to fears regarding letting go. People that are particularly sensitive emotionally need to learn not to take everything personally. If they have allowed themselves to feel hurt it is important not to internalize the hurts and allow them to fester and to build. If this happens the emotional pain grows until it is out of proportion and magnified. Stop replaying the incident over and over in your head. Stop imagining "what ifs." Deal with it quickly then let it go.

The Ball of the Foot

The ball of the foot is where you place your strength. Working with inner strength and pushing forward will clear the things that you feel burden you. The solution is to re-organize what is important to you, to change what is changeable, and to ease what you consider to be burdens. You feel you always have to be "on the ball," but sometimes you feel that as stress. Delegate some of the work. Find ways to release your burdens. When you create tension in this area it's usually a challenge that you created to experience organization and management. This area corresponds to the lungs or breathing in life. Organization will help you to relieve stress and free yourself to enjoy life more fully.

The Top of the Foot

Pain on the top of the foot indicates stress about little things in your home life. Like the saying goes, "don't sweat the small stuff." Let go of the little nuisances. If you feel you must worry, save it for the big things. Challenges that are manifesting may be little things that you find annoying about your partner, things that require attention in your home, or anything that is disturbing your peace of mind.

Notice that I did not say that these were emotional disturbances. This involves your mind. It is your thoughts that are creating the condition. Stop trying to analyze everything. If you feel unsettled or annoyed then do something about it instead of spending your time thinking about making changes. Keep in mind that little things become magnified if you keep thinking of them repeatedly. It is your thoughts that create. If something is bothering you deal with it and don't give it a second thought. I mean that literally. Don't give it a second thought.

My grandmother always said that in marriage we should sleep with our heads on the same pillow. In other words, don't go to bed angry.

That's good advice. However, I am talking about more than just annoyances concerning your partner. I am talking about any little things that disturb the peace in your home. It could be as simple as procrastinating about hanging some curtain rods or cleaning out a closet. When you have chronic pains on the top of the foot there are many little things that you keep on your mind.

Or you keep them on your foot, as the case may be.

It's good to see you can keep your sense of humor.

Now we'll talk about the sides of the foot.

The Sides of the Foot

Do you mean like bunions?

Yes. You're sidestepping issues. Get a grip on the issues and face them squarely. Organize and get yourself working to solve what challenges you are facing. Notice, too, your attitude about meeting challenges. Try to look upon it as a joyous adventure rather than a chore. Every job is beneficial if you have a positive perspective.

I've had a slight bone condition here for years yet I face my challenges.

They're not growing are they?

No.

These were old challenges.

So if they were old challenges, how do I get rid of them?

When you've let it go for so long you may wish to go to a doctor for extra assistance. You must have an absolute knowing in your own healing abilities to heal an area that has grown hard with years of neglect. It is possible and masters have been able to do such healing. There have been few of you that have allowed yourselves that level of belief. However, facing and meeting the new challenges can prevent new growth.

What's the best way to deal with all of these issues?

Meditate on the sore area and find what issues are causing your disease. Daily positive affirmations are helpful. Don't just mumble the affirmation once or twice during the day. I tell you yet again: say your affirmation aloud and with conviction. Place it on your refrigerator, your bathroom mirror, your radio, and where ever you will see it. Repeat it loudly at least three times each time you pass your reminders. Paying attention to what is happening with your emotions will make a difference. When you find you are being hard on yourself or absorbing the stress of others, stop, pay attention, and release the stress.

Meditation will release stress, but what can people do when they are at work?

When you notice that you are beginning to feel stressful and feel your body beginning to tense, stop, take some deep breaths, and consciously relax those areas that were tensing. Do some stretching exercises. The key is being consciously aware of the signals your body is sending you. Meditation does not have to be in a quiet place with soft music and candlelight. You can meditate while looking out of your window, walking in nature, swinging on a porch swing, or watching a butterfly. Don't meditate while you are driving or operating machinery.

Did you wish to give affirmations or exercises to help?

If the foot is what you wish to heal keep in mind that the issues in this area are minor issues. One exercise is to take a few deep breaths and focus on the foot. Relax each toe. Relax the arch. Relax the muscles on top of the foot. Concentrate on the individual areas of the foot. Focus on relaxing all the muscles.

Picture the painful area of the foot bathed in the color red. With your mind strip away all of the red. When the red is completely gone fill that area with a brilliant white-golden light, knowing that the white light is healing the entire area. Let yourself make the healing totally real. Visualize your foot as healed. Picture your self walking, running, or dancing with no difficulties. Make it like a motion picture. Feel how you would feel on perfect healthy feet. Let yourself truly know that healing has taken place. Make yourself totally believe.

Another exercise is looking within. Ask your subconscious to release the information to you. What are the issues that are causing you discomfort in your feet? Go into meditation. Or, before you fall asleep ask your subconscious to release the information to you in a dream that you will remember.

Keep a pad and pencil next to your bed to record your dream upon awakening. Keep a journal. Writing will release information to you. Angels will help you to know the information. Ask for divine guidance, but be prepared to pay attention. Answers are not always immediately given. The answers will always be brought. Look for them. Answers can come in a book, in the newspaper, or as you turn on the television or the radio. You may hear the answer from a friend or a stranger.

Many people ask for guidance but forget to listen or to look for the answers. When people pray I always hear their prayers. I always answer prayers. However, sometimes, the answers are not what that person wants to hear. Sometimes the answer is, "no." Be assured, though, that

I always have the highest good of that person in mind each time I answer.

I wish to add a small additional commentary on the foot before we end this chapter. My Children, please keep in mind that the issues involved here are generally minor issues regardless of how physically painful they might be. The amount of physical pain is not an indicator of the seriousness of the underlying problem. The amount of pain can be an indicator of the amount of time that has elapsed before you deal with the problem.

Some of the issues in the foot area are things that began early in your childhood. I am not blaming you or chastising you for letting these issues continue for such a long time as to have manifested themselves now as very bothersome or debilitating foot conditions. On the contrary, you would not have been expected to deal with some of these issues when you were a child. Children have enough on their plate just dealing with every day occurrences.

If you are reading this book you are probably an adult. Hopefully you have a different perspective on life now and are ready to make the necessary changes to heal yourself on all levels. It is up to you to decide for yourselves. Are you happy with your present conditions? Is it worth doing the work necessary to change your life? Have you the courage to face your fears and to overcome them knowing that to do so will affect your life in ways that you may not even have considered?

I am not telling you what to do. There is no right or wrong here. It is solely a matter of choice. It is a private individual choice that you must make for yourself. If you allow someone else to choose for you, you will not complete the transition because your heart will not be fully in it. The key is to have faith in you as well as in me—to know that you can and are healing yourself. You do have all the power within yourself to accomplish even the most difficult of challenges. I have faith in you—each and every one of you. You can do it!

10

The Longest Leg of the Journey

When a person has pain or problems with legs it's usually an indication to them that there are fear related issues that are holding them back from journeying forward. Let's begin with ankles and work our way up.

The Ankles

If you turn the ankle, have sprains, or torn ligaments, it's an indication of a temporary issue. It's a reluctance to step out on a new adventure.

Couldn't it just be klutziness, like the time I was walking on a beach, talking, and not paying attention to where I was walking? I stepped in a hole and tore the ligaments in my ankle?

Yes, you were pre-occupied and not looking where you were going. However, it was more than clumsiness. There were minor issues you were avoiding at the time. What appeared to be an accident really wasn't. Nothing happens by accident. Most "accidents" are lessons of progression. When something manifests itself within the body it's an indication that there are issues to be examined. Part of your soul knew that you were hesitating about beginning a new venture. Your soul said, "Let's keep the mind pre-occupied and let her have to stop and face what she's been avoiding." So you twisted your ankle.

I wish I had known then the reasons behind the injury. I just turned to conventional medicine—ice and ace bandage. What good is it if one doesn't realize the true intent of the injury?

I understand your question and I will answer it by saying that although you were not aware and "awake" at that time your soul was doing its best to get your attention.

I think today it's much easier to deal with these so-called "accidents" because people are becoming aware that we are each responsible for our own predicaments and experiences.

That is correct and that is precisely why we are writing this book at this time. The populace was not ready for this book before now. This book will simplify the basic issues behind physical ailments.

Healing the ankle requires understanding the causes behind the injury. Sprained ankles will indicate the unwillingness of the person to bend in a given situation. The ankle becomes stiff and muscles pull in its efforts to flow more easily. Physically taping the ankle will lend support. Ice will bring down swelling. However, it is the underlying issues that must be discerned. The issue generally associated with the ankle is unwillingness to step forth through a challenge. When faced with new opportunities or challenges the subconscious mind will set up a situation of inflexibility that corresponds with not walking forward out of emotional fear. The more fear one has, even if it is only on a subconscious level, the more immobilizing the injury to the ankle. The injury could be a sprain, torn ligaments, or even a break. What can one do? Physical relief is what people do first, but fear is still holding one back and will keep the ankle weak and vulnerable. You must deal with the fear. Let's look at ways to handle this.

First and foremost is to establish what the fear really is. Writing the answers to these questions would be beneficial:

1. Why are you afraid to walk forward?

2. What is it that you truly fear?

3. Why do you fear it?

4. What is the opportunity or challenge you are facing?

5. What would be the benefits of meeting this challenge?

6. What are the detriments?

7. How can the detriments be changed to make this opportunity acceptable?

8. How will accepting this opportunity or challenge affect your life?

Look for all positive changes meeting this challenge will bring. Spend time thoroughly thinking this out. Write everything associated with the challenge. Has the fear manifested itself as guilt? Fear of the unknown can be immobilizing, but when the total picture is presented, your fears can be eliminated. Looking within brings all answers to challenges.

Reinforcement with positive affirmations erases fears. Tell yourself positive statements:

1. I am walking forward in joy and happy anticipation.

2. I am excited about working on my new opportunity.

3. This challenge is fun.

4. I am going to be so happy when I have accomplished this project.

5. I deserve and accept the pleasure I will receive from completing this challenge.

Repeat your affirmation frequently during the day. Speak it aloud and in a confidant voice. Place written copies of it where you will see it frequently. Know that whatever situation you face you are exactly where you should be at the right time.

Your spirit has set up the situation for you to experience what it desired for you to know. The conscious mind only sees what is presented but the super-conscious knows what is truly desired. To the conscious mind a situation may seem negative or fearful, but it has been purposely set up for you and will bring about the experience your soul requested if you follow it.

The Calves

Let's move up to the calves. They indicate issues involving loving yourself. Calf injuries should make you rest the leg. Sometimes, lives are so busy that you don't take time to get much needed rest. When you have cramps it's a small reminder not to push yourselves so hard. Relax. Release the tension.

I thought cramps were an indication of a lack of potassium.

Let's just say that if there is a lack of vitamins or minerals within the body you caused those vitamins to leave the body. The physical body works with the various layers of a person to bring whatever change is needed, be it in the body, the mind, or the spirit.

So, what you are saying is that if the body requires rest but is not getting it the body will release vitamins or minerals, get sick, or injure itself to make you rest.

That is exactly what I am saying.

The Shins

When a runner undergoes the pain of shin splints or if one walks into a table, for example, and injures a shin it is a reminder to slow down and "smell the roses." I am not being critical of running, but if the running is to push to an extreme, to run so as not to think, to run as an escape, to test the body's endurance, shin splints are an indication that change is warranted. Walking into something is reminding you to pay attention to the present.

The Knees

The knees are indicators that you are being stiff, stubborn, and inflexible. Is it your pride that holds you back? Is it your ego that is unwilling to allow change? Fear resides in the knee—fear of walking forward, fear of the future, fear of making changes.

If someone has a knee injury how can we heal it without surgery?

First, you must find the underlying reason for the injury. Why are you being so stiff and unbending? How will your life change if you bend? Why are you so afraid of change? Get to the heart of the matter.

Second, you must believe that you can change and that you can heal. Follow the steps given in previous chapters to help your self to heal.

Can one heal a torn cartilage with affirmations or hypnotherapy?

Yes. I repeat: you are able to heal every condition you have created. However, you must have absolute belief that you *can* heal yourself. Then go within to find the true cause of the injury or disease.

The Thighs

Good. Now that we've got that straight let's go to the thighs. Lessons involving the thigh injuries are ones of self-inflictions. When you wish to punish yourselves you injure your thigh. This shows where you feel inadequate or unworthy. It is a place where the self holds lessons of self-esteem.

I thought that was the solar plexus charka or energy center.

It is, but you are also holding esteem in the thigh.

What if we hold excess fat or cellulite there?

Again, it is dealing with issues of self-esteem.

Won't exercise help?

Exercise will tone the muscles, but there are underlying issues with which to be dealt.

What about people with diseases or injuries that eventually atrophy the leg muscles?

That's a good question. What is holding these people from moving forward? Fears can be paralyzing. Or, perhaps, they have chosen this method to have their pre-selected experiences.

What about people who choose to be born with incapacitating or debilitating diseases?

People who are born with such afflictions have chosen them before incarnating. Sometimes they wish to experience an injury such as one they have inflicted on another in a past life.

Sometimes they choose their situation as a gift of love for those around them to experience that which they have chosen, such as being of service to another. It's like Christopher Reeve. His injuries were a great gift of love, hope, and inspiration for many. His soul lovingly chose this moment in a time when he could be of such great service. What love and kindness he gives by teaching as an example. Do not think for a moment that his was an "accident." There are no accidents. He is healing. That, too, is demonstrating belief. When a soul chooses such an experience they can make a much faster progression. They, therefore, choose to have a more difficult incarnation because of its great opportunities.

There are exercises that will help you to heal in the leg area. The following is a meditation:

Begin by closing your eyes and breathing very deeply. Relax your body with each breath. Breathe in through your nose deeper and deeper. Hold the count when you have completely filled your lungs down to your abdomen. As you release the air through your mouth concentrate on releasing any fears, any tension, and any stress or complications. Allow yourself to be totally in the moment. Make it your focus to concentrate on now—this moment. Only concentrate on what is happening in the present moment.

Relax each muscle beginning with the feet. Relax each toe, the arch, and the ankle. Continue focusing on each muscle area as you progress up the legs. Let go of any tension in your calves. Completely relax your knees and thighs. Let yourself release any stress you are holding in your hips, your stomach, your abdomen, and your chest. Concentrate on releasing all tension and relaxing each vertebra and muscle as you move from the tail-bone all the way up your back to your neck. Relax your shoulders and neck. Let go of any stress you are carrying there. Feel the relaxation flowing down all the muscles in your arms and your hands. Let your face completely relax. Let go of any tension in your jaw, your facial muscles, your forehead, and your scalp. Your entire body should feel totally relaxed.

Allow your mind to sojourn to your favorite place where you feel at total peace. It could be a place that you remember visiting or it could be a place in your imagination. You might go to the beach or to a peaceful mountaintop. You may find yourself in a beautiful garden. Just know that you are completely safe, secure, and protected. It is your special place where no one else may enter unless invited. Sit down and just "be."

This is the time to let your mind be free to feel and to truly experience your location. Feel water or breeze, smell any sweet flowers, touch the soft grass or sand of the earth, and hear the birds chirping or the wind rustling the leaves of the trees. Look at the beautiful blue sky. Maybe there is a fluffy white cloud drifting overhead. Allow yourself to totally experience your surroundings.

Turn around. You see a path behind you and you begin to walk along the path. Look at the beautiful flowers along the sides of the path. They are all the colors in the rainbow. Notice the majestic trees that line the route—strong, upright trees with leaves that shade and shimmer as they rustle in the gentle breeze. As you look up you see a blue sky peeping through the leaves. The sun is shining. It's a wonderful day for a walk. The temperature is perfect and you feel so comfortable. Continue to walk along and enjoy the smell of the flowers.

Look ahead and you will see a glint of crystal at the end of the path. As you continue along a crystal temple begins to take shape before you. You approach the temple and see a staircase in front of you. On the staircase is a figure robed in white descending to greet you. You know that it is an angel. He reaches out and hands you a robe of the palest violet which you don. You tie it with a silver cord. When this is complete the angel reaches out and gently takes your hand and leads you up the crystal stairs.

In front of you is a great golden door. At a wave of the angel's hand the door opens and you see a large courtyard. You remove your shoes and enter through the portal. As you walk around the courtyard you feel how soft the grass is beneath your feet.

Around the walls are beautiful climbing vines with brightly colored flowers. There are plants of all sizes. You can smell the aroma of sweet herbs. You notice many pedestals around the perimeter are topped with containers of burning incense. Many people are walking around quietly chatting.

Looking around you notice three doors leading to three special rooms. The first door is the entrance to a room of physical healing. The second is a room of mental healing. The third is a room of emotional healing. Your angel leads you into the room that is most appropriate at this time.

As you enter you notice the walls are made of a clear crystal. You can see beautiful colors in every hue shimmering and shining in the walls. Within the room is a plush white lounge chair. Walk over and sit down. It is more comfortable than any chair upon which you have ever been seated. Allow yourself sink into its softness and to totally relax. You know that complete healing is beginning to take place as you relax. Both you and your angel are here to help you to heal.

If you have a physical ailment and are in the first room your angel now displays a large picture of you in front of you. Find the area in your body that requires healing. What does the pain look like? See the pain. Make it visible. Give it a color, a shape, or a sound. What must you do to release the pain or discomfort? Let your imagination show you how to vanquish the distressed area.

Look to your right and you will see a huge cabinet. Within its shelves contains whatever you need as a tool to help you. Stand up and walk over to the cabinet. Your angel opens the doors and tells you to pick out anything you wish from the cabinet that would help you to release the disease. What tool or tools would it take to fix or to erase your ailment? Use your creativity. Make the necessary adjustments. Take your time. Know that healing is indeed taking place in your body simultaneously as you wield your tools on the picture.

If you have gone into the room to deal with mental ailments you notice that there is a computer next to the lounge chair. Turn to the keyboard and type your name. If your problem is caused by a chemical imbalance the screen will automatically show you two pictures of your brain. Look to the left. Any areas of chemical imbalance will be shown colored in red. To the right is the second diagram of your brain as it should look when balanced. Click on a white healthy corresponding area of your brain to capture it. Using your mouse move the healthy section over the affected red area on your unbalanced brain. Do this with each section until your brain looks clean, white, and healthy

If your problem is related to the electrical connections in the brain a picture of your brain will appear showing the electrical circuitry. Join any loose connections by clicking and dragging your mouse. If your brain shows you a tumor use your mouse and the delete key to erase it. Let yourself feel healed. Know that you have made changes in your brain as you have made changes on the computer.

If you have gone into the third room to heal your emotions know that your angel will work with you in complete privacy. This is the room in which you can be completely honest. No thoughts or feelings may be hidden here. You will not be judged. You will not be criticized. No matter what you say or feel you are unconditionally loved here.

Your angel sits in another white lounge chair facing you and waits to really listen to you. Open your heart. Don't hold anything back. Tell your angel exactly what you are feeling. Relate any experiences, no matter how shameful or humiliating, that have hurt you and are impacting your present feelings. Don't be afraid to cry or to yell. Nothing you say to your angel will leave this room. Let your angel help you to release your emotional burdens. Take as much time as you need. When you have completely unburdened yourself your angel hugs you in his embrace and you let yourself feel the wonder and peace of his love.

It is time to follow your angel to the exit. Notice how much you feel changed. You *know* that healing has taken place. Allow yourself to feel joyful, freer, and lighter as you put your shoes back on and hand your robe back to your angel. Leave the courtyard, pass through the golden doors, and descend the stairs of the crystal temple.

As you walk confidently back toward the path your angel walks next to you and tells you what you will have coming into your life in the near future. Take a few minutes to speak with your angel. When you are finished talking continue walking back on the path that leads you home. You may return to the crystal temple any time you wish. Now, though, it is time to say goodbye to your angel.

At the count of three you will awaken and feel totally refreshed like you've just had a long nap. One, beginning to feel your body sitting in your seat, two, starting to move your hands or feet, stretching your neck and three, when you are ready, opening your eyes, stretching, and feeling totally aware, alert, and healthy.

That which truly holds a person back from total healing is the degree of his faith. He must have faith in himself and in his own abilities to heal as well as faith in me. This is an interesting challenge for those who choose it. You make it so complex, but it's really very simple.

Simple isn't always easy.

It's only difficult if you make it so. Can you not see that fear is at the root of your difficulties? What is it that you fear?

It could be a fear of success. If we are successful it will bring change. That can be very fearful. Or it could be a fear of failure. If we meditate, say affirmations, or visualize and still see no changes it reinforces our fears. I know that underlying what we do are thoughts that it really won't work or that nothing has ever changed before, so why should this time be different. How do we reach the point of absolutely knowing that what we do will effectively heal whatever we desire?

That is the key to self-healing. You must absolutely *know* without any reservation that you are able to heal yourself and anyone else who is ready to be healed. The only one who is holding you back is you. You are the only one who can achieve the absolute belief necessary to do the kind of healing for which you are constantly asking. Do you not think that you would have such a compelling desire to do healing if I had not given you the ability to do so? Of course you have such ability. You have used that ability in many lifetimes. Your challenge this lifetime is to remember how powerful you really are—to remember that you can heal yourself and anyone who asks for help. It is you who make this a difficult challenge.

Challenges do not have to be difficult. They can be quite simple. You keep forgetting that what you consider to be reality is really all an illusion—your body, your diseases, and your challenges. That is not what is real. It is your spirit's desire to experience these things. Your spirit loves all of it—the drama, the emotion, the challenges—everything. It is you who created the fear. What is fear but "False Evidence Appearing Real?" What is it that you really fear? Is it that you can't heal as you wish? Of course you can. Is it that you will appear foolish in front of other people? Go on, take a chance. Show to yourself as well as to other people that it can be done. Past masters have led by example. Allow yourself to remember that you, too, are such a master. Let go of your fears and doubts.

Be who you truly are. That is the key to life. Just be who you are, all of you. It's as simple as that. It's only difficult if you make it so. It can be easy if you make it so. Change your attitude. Change your self talks. Be positive. Know that your abilities are unlimited. Know that you can do anything if you set your mind to it.

I used to feel that way when I was young but it seems that the older I get the more doubtful I get. I am sure that it must be the same for many of us. As we age there come more experiences. The more failures I experience the more my doubts are reinforced. How can we learn from past failures and know in our hearts that the next time we try will be different—that the next time we will succeed?

Okay. I see that I have to go over this yet again. Every day is a new beginning. Every attempt at anything is a new attempt. Do you think that scientists get frustrated and doubtful every time that they fail? On the contrary, it makes them happy and hopeful because they know that each time they fail, that's one more thing that they can cross off of their list of things to try. That is one step closer to finding a solution.

It's all a question of attitude. It doesn't matter what you are attempting to accomplish or in what area of your life—physical healing, emotional healing, relationships, or spiritual evolution. Bless each supposed failure because it is bringing you one step closer to your goal. You can see that it really is not a failure at all. It is growth. It is strength to keep trying. It is just another step along the path. So push up your sleeves, bless the attempt, and go back to work with a renewed sense of purpose. Be positive. Be loving to yourself. Be who you are. Be me. Believe.

I would like to end this chapter with a few words more on being fearful of making "strides" on your evolutionary path. Aches and pains in your legs are your physical manifestations of your fears concerning "walking your path." You are all walking your path—every day, every hour, and every minute. You cannot *not* be on your path. That would be impossible. The question is: how fast do you choose to evolve? That is strictly up to you. Some of you that are now walking the earth plane are very advanced. You, my love, are very advanced.

Do I really wish to put that in writing for others to read?

Why not? That is one of your fears rising to the surface. Why do you not just accept who you are? That is what I have been trying in these dialogues to instill in our readers. Just accept who you are. *Be* who you are. If you are not where you wish to be at this moment *be* who you wish to be. Just be the person who acts lovingly, kindly, and considerately if that is who you choose to be.

Some of you have barely touched the surface of the person you really are. Many of you are walking around in a dreamlike state. You are barely conscious of your thoughts, your words, or your actions. The majority of you are becoming aware some of the time. However, your conscious awareness takes a backseat to your everyday lives. You are so concerned with the daily events in your outer world that you spend precious little time working on your inner world. Yes, you meditate *some* of the time. Yes, you pay attention to your thoughts and words *some* of the time.

Most of the time, you spend thinking of your daily activities, your family, or your work. I realize that these things are important to you. What I am suggesting is that you consider every moment to be of the utmost importance to you. I have given you each moment as a "present." That is where you should be living—in the present. For in reality, that is the only place in which you can live. Treat every moment as if it were your last. How would you speak to each person if you knew that these words would be the last time you spoke? So many of you lament that you never expressed your love or never said how you felt to a person before he left your world. How would you treat yourself if you knew you were leaving? (I did not say dying because in fact you cannot die. You are eternal. You merely change form.) Would you not be more appreciative of the beauty of nature around you? Would you not be kinder to yourself? Would you not act more lovingly to your family, friends, or peers?

Pay attention to each moment if you choose to evolve more quickly. When you are driving in your car and someone cuts you off, what are you doing to yourself by becoming angry? Does it solve any of your problems to become enraged? Does it get you to your destination any faster? What would be the more loving thing for you to do?

It is totally up to you how you will react in every situation. I am not criticizing I am merely observing and making suggestions. The next time your child breaks some household item, how will you react? If this were the last time you were going to see your child again, now, how would you react? Before falling back on your old patterns like yelling or saying hurtful things, stop, breathe, and be the person that you would like to be. This may actually take some conscious effort on your part.

Are we being a little sarcastic here?

I am just a bit. It truly is only to show you how most of you think. If you choose to become aware or if you choose to become a master it will take some conscious effort on your part to change those old patterns that no longer serve you. It's not difficult to form new patterns that will take you where you wish to go.

The masters are consistent in their thoughts and their behaviors. They are no different from you. However, they know the secret: you and I are one. That being so, you being God, how would we react now in every day situations? Have I not infinite patience? Have I not abundant and infinite love? Are you not part of me? Therefore, does it not follow that you, too, have an endless supply of love? Of course you do. Most of you feel separated from me and separated from my love. I say to you: go forth in love. Go forth in confidence. Go forth on strong healthy legs. We are truly one and the same. You can *never* be alone for I am *always* with you—all ways.

11

The Hips and The Stomach

<u>The Hips</u>

I will divide the torso into sections because it's very complex. Let's begin with the hips. When a person is weak in the hip area it is an indication that they are very discontent with the work they are pursuing. To have stiffness or arthritis in the hips shows the person that change is needed. Most people stuff frustration or anger from work into the hips.

There are several ways work-related fear manifests in the hips. It can be as fat or as stiffness.

Yes. Fat is an indication that the person feels that he or she needs protection and insulation with an extra layer of fat. Fat is just a physical manifestation of fear.

Stiffness is an indication that what is feared is change. Change can be in the work place, the work itself, forced retirement, being laid off, or even changes in working companions or bosses. Looking to be safe is hardly considered an issue in companies today. Job security seems to be a non-expectation.

Look how many youngsters are the bosses. Yes, they are creative. Yes, they can make very good business executives. However, in the process, the life skills and experience of the elders should not be ignored or removed. A better solution is for younger executives to sit down with senior workers and to learn from them. Generally, their knowledge is valuable both in the work place and in personal and people skills.

What if someone is forced into retirement? Their resentment and frustration can manifest itself in sore hips or even just bruising hips by repeat-

edly walking into tables. What can be done to alleviate the dis-ease in this area?

That's a good question. A substitute should be found. So, you are retired. You feel that you have nothing to look forward to. Why not begin to do all those things you have always wanted to do but never found time to do because you were working?

What about people on a small fixed income?

There are many free things. Volunteer to help others or get a small part-time job. Take courses. Teach courses. Take advantage of the free lectures or activities.

It seems to be a circle. You resent your situation so you bring on a pain that can be debilitating. Now you have the time to change your lifestyle and do the fun things, but your bodily pains are restricting you from enjoying doing these activities. What can we do to eliminate the physical diseases so that we can enjoy doing all of the things we wish?

Good. I am seeing you wish to have practical exercises that will help to release the hip discomfort. I will suggest looking to what is your real fear:

1. What will your life hold for you now that you have the freedom and time to do whatever you desire?

2. Is it the lack of structure that frightens you?

3. Will it mean not having the provisions that a regular income provides?

4. Will you lack social contact?

5. Do your days look endlessly empty? Do you need activities to keep you busy? Let yourself find the real fear.

6. Will you no longer have an important position where people look up to you and listen to you?

7. Are you losing your position of control or power?

8. Will you no longer feel needed?

Take a good look at the next year, five years, or ten years. How can you fill that time productively? Perhaps it is finally time to work on your spiritual growth. Travel. Read. Don't let your mind atrophy. Most of you stop feeding your mind in your thirties. Keep your mind active. Take classes. Teach classes. Walk in the woods. Play a sport. Do you really think that just because your youth oriented company no longer appreciates your knowledge and wisdom that there are not many places that really need you? Make your life fun by doing all the things you have wished to do.

This is fine emotionally, but will it alleviate the physical pain?

As I have mentioned elsewhere in this book, you created your pains and discomforts on some level and you do have the ability to relieve them and to heal. The key is to have total belief in your ability to heal yourself. Until you reach the point of absolute knowing medicine provides pain relievers as temporary aids.

So far you've been discussing seniors. There are younger people who have problems with their hips, too.

Of course this is true. What do you think has brought on their challenge?

It must be fear, also. Pain can indicate a need for attention. Pain can suggest a control issue. Pain can allude to a desired experience as a carry-over from a past life. Fat can be protection from physical attention. Fat concerns complicated love issues related to self-love as well as the love from others.

Excellent. You have been paying attention. All of these are very valid reasons for hip aliments or extra pounds on the hips. Everything boils down to fear. Completely release the fears and you can release the ailment. Learn to love your hips. Learn to love your entire body. It's truly miraculous in all of its functions.

The Stomach

Stomach issues range from digestive disorders to cancer to fat. Let's begin with digestive disorders. How are you digesting ideas? Do you stubbornly hold on to old ideas or are you open to new suggestions and new thoughts? Where do you generally get your ideas? How many of you are truly creative thinkers? The majority of you do not think for yourselves. You have adopted the thoughts of your parents, teachers, ministers, or peers. When was the last time you had a truly original thought? Are you sure that you didn't read that idea somewhere or hear it from another and adapt it for your own? You accept the thoughts of others even if they are difficult to digest. Do you find yourself with flatulence or gas pains? What about expressing your opinions? Does confrontation, public speaking, or expressing yourself in a group "tie your stomach into knots?" What does confronting your boss or co-workers do to your stomach? Are you swallowing aggression, anger, or hurt? Does that not churn in your stomach? Is that becoming extra fat?

How can we confront people or speak in public without getting a nervous stomach?

What are the fears behind those activities? If you are fearful of confrontation what is it that scares you? Are you afraid of losing your job? Are you afraid someone will criticize or belittle you? Are you afraid of a physical confrontation? Consider changing your approach to that person. Speak calmly, quietly, and respectfully. Ask instead of demand. Try buffering criticism with compliments. Speak gently and lovingly. Speak to him or her as you would like him to speak to you.

Create your environment to your satisfaction. You can't change your boss or peers; but you can change your attitude towards them. Are you giving unsolicited advice or direction? Why do you give away your energy? If you allow yourself to become upset are you not fueling the power of that person to upset you? Are you not encouraging that person to control you? Keeping in mind that I created all of you with equal importance why do you allow yourself to be intimidated? If you feel that you lack education, take some classes. Become more proficient in your field. With practice comes confidence. Practice your craft. Practice your people skills. Practice loving yourself. Practice being the person you would like to be. Soon you will find that you have become that person.

These suggestions are applicable for public speaking as well. Know your subject proficiently. Know your audience. Practice your speech to the mirror over and over until you are comfortable with it. When you give your speech remember that your audience regards you as knowledgeable. They are not there to criticize or to find fault with you. They are interested in what you have to say. You have value to them. Knowing that you were the person requested to speak, let yourself feel worthy of that honor. Teaching is a gift you give to others. If your speech is an introduction for another, consider the honor you do to that speaker by your introduction. When you consider the others you lose your own fears.

As for the stomach being constipated are you "stuck" in your old ways and beliefs? Are you "stuck" in the past? What are you so tightly holding on to? If you frequently have diarrhea from what are you running? Fears make such an impact on the body.

Be realistic about this. Look at your diet, too. Are you consuming foods that are difficult to digest or that are binding? If you eat a large dish of prunes you will find yourself in the bathroom. Be aware of your nutritional habits. Perhaps all you need to relieve your stomach disorder is a change of diet. Relieving the emotional or mental concern aids healing but be practical, too. How frequent are your stomach problems? Is this a chronic problem or an occasional problem? When did the problem begin? What was happening in your life at that time? How has this affected your state of mind?

I discussed in the introductory chapter diseases such as cancer. I mention it here to note that stomach or colon cancer is in the area of the third chakra. Look at the issues embodied in this energy center; they are related to personal power. How healthy is your self-esteem?

Do you love and respect yourself? Do you even like yourself? Do you believe in yourself and your intuition?

Why have you been holding onto anger, resentment, or hurt so long in this area that it has begun to "eat away" at you? Do you even know what emotions have been buried so deeply or has your mind tried to dismiss them as a self-defense mechanism? It is possible that this disease has come into your life as a spiritual challenge? Consider that one. I am not saying that any of these considerations or inner work is a substitute for conventional medical treatment. I am only saying that self-healing is possible based on your belief system. Is there any reason why conventional medicine and self-exploration cannot work faster simultaneously? Do you not think that modern medical knowledge and technology has been inspired from me?

What can you do to avoid diseases of this area?

First, I would suggest that you give major consideration to strengthening your relationship with yourself. Look at your gifts and talents. Note your positive qualities. Stop criticizing or condemning yourself. You are good enough, beautiful enough, smart enough, and talented enough. You don't have to be perfect; that's my job. You are worth being loved. You are worth loving, respecting, and knowing yourself. Why do you let the opinions and criticisms of others influence your opinion of yourself? Your opinions and ideas are just as valid as those of another.

Continue repeating those positive self-talks. If you are not content at this moment with the person you are look to see where change would be beneficial. What kind of person would you like to be? It does not matter who you have been or what you have done up to this point. You can change. You can develop loving qualities. You have already taken the first step; you are reading this book.

Second, and very importantly, learn to release your anger or your hurt quickly. People have a tendency to hold onto their old injuries. They use them as excuses to refuse commitments, to seem the martyr, or to receive pity. This is like flogging a dead horse. The past is gone. If you are serious about healing your life deal with the past then let it go. Learn to really forgive both others and yourself. By holding onto anger or old emotional wounds you give them more energy. Eventually they will begin to appear within your physical body if they are not eliminated. Methods to release anger and pain are discussed in the chapter about letting go of physical and emotional bonds. Do this for yourself. Then teach your children how to deal with anger or pain without harming others or themselves.

12

Ouch, My Aching Lower Back

I would like to mention at the onset of this discourse that pain is actually very positive. It indicates to you where you have issues with which you should deal. It affords you the opportunity to change and to grow. So bless pain instead of cursing it. There is always a reason for the pain. When that reason is so worrisome that it limits your physical abilities it is time to deal with it.

The complete body is a wondrous instrument. God created humans as a beautiful but complex work. Here is how life functions:

Man has a thought.

That thought, if repeated often enough, becomes a belief.

That belief is implanted within the subconscious mind. It is left there until a situation is created that requires that belief to surface.

The belief manifests itself first in the ego. This is where it's necessary to change this belief if it's negative. When you hear yourself speaking negatively, do whatever is necessary to turn that belief around to positive.

What happens when the belief is not changed is that it begins to move from the ego to the astral or emotional body. (The various layers of the body are discussed in the chapter on belief.)

Once the belief enters the astral body it's able to grow by enhancing it with emotions.

When it grows large enough, it moves to the etheric body. This is the aura or energy field that people can see around a person. Here we can actually see tears that can be made by these negative beliefs.

When the tears become large enough the belief becomes manifest in the physical body. Now you must deal not only with changing the faulty belief but also with healing the emotions associated with that belief. You must also repair the auric field and heal the physical pain, discomfort, or disease that has been created within the physical body.

Let's begin with an example of how this works. Many people have been complaining about lower back pain. Let's take a financial thought since that is one issue that affects the lower back area.

Thought: I can't make enough money.
Underlying thoughts could be:

> I'm not educated enough to get a better job.
> My boss doesn't appreciate my value.
> I must work overtime to meet my financial needs or get a second job.
> If I support a family I have no money or time left over to do extra things that I would enjoy doing.

Belief: I'll never receive the salary that I would really like to get.
Underlying beliefs:

> I'll never be rich.
> I'm not smart enough to be paid a six-figure salary.
> I'll buy a lottery ticket, but I'll never win. Someone has to win, though, so I will keep buying a ticket even though in the back of my mind I know I really won't win.
> I can't get a break.
> I can't find the right job.
> This is the way life is so just accept it.
> Let's just do the work and try to pay the bills.

Now this belief moves into the astral or emotional body.
Underlying emotions:

> I'm upset and worried that I won't have enough money to pay all
> of my bills. The credit card debts are accruing a lot more interest
> on top of what I owe. How can I pay off my debts?
> I'm nervous and scared.
> It makes me feel frustrated and angry that I am not appreciated at
> my job.
> It upsets me that people much younger are being promoted over
> me or making a fortune while I am just making ends meet.
> I am feeling guilty because I can't give my family all the extras I
> would like.
> I am depressed because I don't like my job, boss, co-workers, or
> hours.

Now there are tears starting in the etheric body. When the tears
become large enough the beliefs begin to enter the physical body.
When beliefs enter the body they manifest in the areas of your energy
centers or their corresponding parts.

Each energy center has its own issues with which the body has to
deal. This applies, likewise, to the corresponding area in the body. In
the case of lower back pain financial issues must be dealt with in the
second chakra energy center. This is not to say that the pain in the
back is not very real. By this time it has become a very real pain. Usually this is the area in which a person is feeling very unsupported at
their work place or at home. We realize that the times are not always
opportune for changing work positions. It is not always easy to get a
new job or to be promoted in your present job—unless it is. So many
people opt for the security of staying in their present position no matter the upset.

How do you begin to release the back pain? Make note of when you
are feeling the back pain. Does it occur randomly or when you are
doing a particular activity? Does it occur when you have been sitting

still for long periods of time? Pains do not occur just because of deep-seated emotional problems. Be practical and logical. Are you giving your back adequate support in the chair you have chosen? Have you been lifting heavy weights using your leg muscles rather than your back muscles? Do you do stretching exercises before and after a strenuous activity? There are very logical reasons as to why you are feeling a temporary soreness in your back.

Applying cold or heat can alleviate soreness. You don't have to analyze every ache or pain. If you have a chronic pain then it may be worth your while to determine the original cause. A doctor can show you the physical cause of your pain. You may have ruptured a disc or injured another part of your spine. However, what a doctor does not do for you is to show you why you caused that injury.

I know that you will argue that you were injured, for example, in a car accident. It wasn't your fault. The other car ran a light and hit you. I tell you this again: there are no accidents. Everything happens for a reason. Many happenings are pre-determined. Your soul leads you into circumstances that afford you the experiences that you have selected. A doctor can help you to heal a physical pain but if you have not completed your experience, is it not logical that a pain can re-occur in the area of your unsettled issues? Pain is your soul's way of showing you that you need to be more aware.

As mentioned earlier a place to begin is in relaxation. Sit with your legs propped up with a pillow beneath your knees. Make sure your back is supported in a comfortable position. Close your eyes. Breathe deeply and concentrate on breathing rhythmically and slowly. Let your mind focus on the area of the lower back.

Ask your subconscious mind to release to you the real reason that it is manifesting physical pain. What should come are words or thoughts flashing through your mind, a picture, or feelings that will indicate your challenge. Try to see where the belief originated. What are your real feelings? Once the true beliefs have been ascertained they can be eradicated or changed.

I present to you the following meditation that will be of help to change negative beliefs: Sit in a comfortable chair or lie down if you are sure that you will not fall asleep. Let your eyes gently close. Take several deep breaths. Breathe in through your nose, completely filling your chest all the way down through your abdomen. Hold that breath for a few counts then exhale through your mouth. As you exhale know that you are releasing any tension and any stress. Scan your body for any areas that feel tension. Consciously relax each tight area. Allow yourself to go farther and farther into total relaxation.

In your mind's eye see in front of you a beautiful meadow. You can feel a gentle breeze caressing your hair. You look up and see that the sky is a beautiful clear blue. The sun is shining and it gently warms your face. You can remove your shoes and feel the soft green grass beneath your feet. There are wildflowers of every color you can imagine, and they are so beautiful. Their sweet smell wafts upward for you to enjoy. You hear birds singing sweetly in a nearby tree. You may see colorful butterflies as they flit around you and tickle the flowers.

In the center of the meadow is a large castle. Approach the doorway. Open the door and look inside. Hanging on a peg just inside the portal is a lantern. You take up this lantern and notice that in front of you is a spiral stone staircase heading downward. You begin to walk on this staircase holding the lantern ahead of you so that your way is completely lighted. This is a special private staircase. You are completely secure, completely protected, and completely safe. You continue down this staircase, spiraling downward, around and around, going farther and farther down into the castle.

At the bottom of the staircase you see a large door. The door has any decoration on it that you wish; or it could be a plain door. You notice that hanging next to the door is a large key. Take the key, unlock the door, and find yourself stepping into a comfortable room. There is a large over-stuffed chair in the center of the room. Go over to it and sit down. It is the most comfortable chair you have ever been in and you totally relax. As you begin to look around the room you see that next to the chair is an end table. On it are many pens of different colors. To the left is a wall with a fireplace and there is a beautiful crackling warm welcoming fire glowing there.

Straight ahead of you is a large bookcase. On the shelves are your books of beliefs. These are your books about your life. Stand up and walk over to the bookcase. There are many books from which to choose. There is a book of relationships, a book of weight loss, a book of fun, a book of creativity, and many more. Today you pull the book of finances or the book of beliefs that is affecting your current condition.

Take the book over to the stuffed chair. Sit down once again and place the book on your lap. Look down at the front cover. Notice what it says. What color is it? How is it decorated? Open the book. As you flip through the pages they will automatically stop at the page at which you will see the negative belief that you have regarding your present situation. What does it say? It might say something like, "I'm not smart enough to have a high paying position." Look at the end table next you and you will see a large black magic marker. Pick it up and draw a large "X" over the words on the page. Now put the marker down and tear off that page from the book. Take that sheet of paper and tear it into many small pieces. Put the book down. Stand up and walk over to the fireplace. Throw the pieces of paper into the fire and watch them as they burn leaving only ashes that go right up the chimney as sparks.

Now go back to the chair and pick up the book. Look at the pages. If the belief was so great that it made marks onto the next few pages, repeat the process. Make an "X" on each page, tear it out of the book, shred it into little pieces, and burn them in the fire. Continue doing this until you come to a page in the book that is completely blank and clean.

Turn to the end table and pick up a pen of any color you wish. It could be gold, silver, bronze or any color, and write your new positive belief in your book of beliefs. "I am smart enough to have any position I wish." Or write what ever is appropriate for you.

Continue through the book following this procedure with any other faulty negative thoughts. Make and "X." Rip out the page. Tear it into little pieces and burn them. Write your new positive thought on the next clean page. When you have finished take your book of beliefs and put it back on your library shelf. You know that you may return to this room at any time you wish in meditation.

Walk out of the room and lock the door. This is your private room, your private library. Put the key back on the peg knowing that it is perfectly safe and that no one else will ever touch it. Take up your lantern and proceed up the spiral stone staircase, climbing round and round, higher and higher up through the castle, higher and higher until you come to the door leading out of the castle. Place the lantern back on the peg and walk out through the door leaving it closed.

Ahead of you see the meadow that will take you back home. It is a magnificent day. The temperature is perfect—not too hot and not too cold. You proceed back across the meadow breathing in the clean fresh air, looking up at the blue of the sky, maybe whistling or singing along with the birds, and enjoying the beautiful flowers. Perhaps you see some animals along the way. There may be little chipmunks, butterflies, or deer. You feel lighter already knowing that you have changed. Know that things in your workplace will begin to change because you now have a new attitude, new beliefs, and you feel a new excitement.

At the count of three you will begin to feel yourself back in your seat. One, two, feeling your physical body, and three, when you are ready and only when you are ready, opening your eyes, stretching, smiling, and feeling totally alert, totally aware, and totally awake.

I would like to continue discussing issues other than financial ones that can be held in the lower back. This area also holds issues of creativity, security, relationships, and sexuality.

Let's begin with creativity.

Creativity involves all aspects of life. A mother who is staying at home to raise her children must be just as creative in the raising of those children as an artist, a writer, a doctor, a technician, or anyone else. When one loves his job and does it whole-heartedly he incorporates at least a modicum of creativity. There are many jobs that require repetition, and it is easy for boredom to quickly overtake the doer. However, if a person is creative he can pass his time more constructively. Find ways to make the tedium more interesting. Play mental games with yourself. For example, Love, I know that you do this when you do a job that you consider to be boring. You do this every time that you iron shirts. You play mental games with colors and fabric patterns. You even try to match hangers. Anyone can find creative ways to make a job more interesting.

Let's continue by discussing another issue that can be physically manifested in the area of the lower back. This is one of sexuality.

Sexuality issues can go back to early childhood. They can even be carried over from past life experiences. From his earliest time a child receives negative input about his body. His natural instinct is to pleasurably touch himself. Each time he does, however, his parents admonish him and tell him that that is unacceptable behavior.

As the child grows he has a natural curiosity about sex. However, he receives very mixed messages. Television, radio, magazines, or movies, all give the message that sex is fun, that sex is power, and that casual sex is acceptable. At the same time parents, teachers, and ministers try to teach youngsters that sex is taboo until they are adults. Most parents can't even discuss sex with their children and prefer to leave that topic to the schools. Parents rarely demonstrate their natural desire for closeness in front of their children. They hide their bodies and feel embarrassed to be seen naked in front of their children.

In societies where sex is accepted as part of the natural condition there is little rape or sexual abuse. There are no prostitutes or sexual deviates. Who has mandated what is abhorrent and unnatural behavior anyway? In many societies there is no shameful hiding of natural instincts. Why do you think that I made sex so pleasurable if I did not mean for you to enjoy it? Do you notice that these societies that follow the natural instincts that I have given you are the ones that you call uncivilized? Is it civilized to use sex as a weapon? Is it civilized to use sex as a control issue? Is it civilized to use sex to create feelings of shame, humiliation, violation, punishment, or power?

When you are frequently hurting in your lower back ask yourself what your feelings are concerning sex. What were you taught as a child? Have you released any negative teachings? Do you still feel inhibited or shameful? Or perhaps, you have rebelled and have frequent hedonistic meaningless sex? If you are still holding issues from childhood for how long to you wish to carry them? Sex was meant to be pleasurable not a burden or an obligation. Nor was it meant to become a consuming issue with its frequency.

Deep seated feelings concerning sex can even be carried over from past life experiences. I know that there are still many skeptics who doubt that they have lived prior lives. I tell you this: you all have lived many lives. There have been so many books written detailing past lives that have been substantiated and verified that I do not have to go deeply into that subject. Look to your feelings of deja vu. Look to your dreams for flashes of past lives. Look to your feelings of knowing that you know someone even though you have just met. Look to your feelings that you can trust a particular stranger or that you instinctively don't like someone even though that person has done nothing to antagonize you. Look to your feelings that you know a place even when you have not visited it before. If you are drawn to a new place or repelled by it, trust your instincts. Trust your feelings.

All of your past experiences are stored in your subconscious mind. They rise to the surface as feelings when triggered by a particular person, place, sight, smell, or sound. Is it not the time to conquer your fears? Is it not the time to release your inhibitions? Is it not the time to explore who you really are? I am not here to tell you what to do. It is your choice whether to heal your conditions or to continue as you are doing. There is no right or wrong. You decide if you are content with things as they are.

I would like to say a few words to those of you who complain about pain from the lower back that extends along the sciatic nerve.

Sciatic pain indicates deeper fears. The issues here are so fearful that they are restraining you from moving forward. What are the monetary issues that are creating a fearful future? You may have strong security issues that are being held in your lower back. Some of you have created a lack of money. Are you afraid to be independent? Are you afraid to be powerful? Are you afraid to be in control? Do you have a need for others to pity you? Are you afraid of change?

I can hear arguments already. How have I created a lack of money? I can't find a job. No one will hire me because I am too old, too young, too inexperienced, too thin, or too fat. My job only pays minimum wage. I can't get a break, and so on and so forth. I tell you this: you have drawn your situation to you either by your attitude or for the experience you intended to have.

There is a law of attraction that I have put into place in the universe. If you are sending out negative vibrations then that is what you will draw back to yourself. If you are sending out positive vibrations you will draw positive things into your life. "But," you say, "I am willing to work. I even hold down two jobs to make ends meet." To you I say, "Yes, that you are a hard worker is commendable, but what is your underlying belief?" It is the underlying beliefs that are holding you back. These are the beliefs that you feel are true deep down in your mind. These are truths that you may not admit to anyone else. You may not even admit them to yourself. Usually they are truths dealing with unworthiness, self-esteem, and love.

Let's analyze this. Are these really truths? Are they not just the things that have been told to you from your childhood? Who in your life made you feel so unworthy? Did people make you feel that if you did not produce or were perfect then they would not love you? Who kept repeating to you that you would never amount to anything or that you were stupid? Most likely these things were taught to you from your parents or family, your teachers, your peers, or your ministers. I say to you: why do you keep buying into these negative thoughts now that you are an adult? Just because you were taught to believe these things as a child does not make them true. Just because someone else tells you something does not make it true for you. Is it not time for you to start thinking for yourself instead of accepting the thoughts of others?

I created each of you as unique individuals with unique gifts and talents. You each have whatever abilities you need to be the best person that you are. I did not make one person better or worthier than another. It is up to you to decide who you are by the choices that you make.

You can have whatever it is that you truly wish to have, but you must totally believe that you can have it. I never said that only the poor would enter heaven. That is nonsense. Everyone enters heaven. In reality there is no place else to go. There is no hell. Hell is somewhere that was created by your churches to control people by the use of fear. If someone believes that he will go to hell when he dies then that is what his mind creates. I tell you that any time he wishes to come home to me I will always accept all of my children with love.

Your monetary status is not important to me. Whether you have chosen to be a king or a homeless person is not important to me. So live your life as you wish. You may have all of the toys or you may have none of the toys. It is your choice. If your present beliefs are not serving you then change them.

I will close the discussion on the lower back area with this thought: make time to study your present situation. I would suggest that you do this at a time when you are not in pain. Most people seem to have a harder time concentrating on things other than the actual pain while they are hurting. Look at where you are. Look at what has brought you to your present condition. Look at where you would like to be in your future. Then make the choices that will bring you to that place. Change your thoughts, your beliefs, and your attitude if they no longer serve you. There are suggestions throughout this book of how to make changes in your life.

13

Half-Way There (The middle back)

Tonight we will work with the middle of the back which encompasses the third chakra or energy center. People generally think of the chakras in front of the body but forget that they extend behind you. They are like a disk attached to a funnel that goes through the center of the body and back out onto a disk again. You will remember that the third chakra deals with issues of self-esteem. You carry the majority of emotional issues here. What issues are generally in the rear chakra are very emotional. The fear is dealing with self-love and self-disempowerment. Issues of self-power are carried in the stomach.

On occasion your back aches, doesn't it? At times you feel like your back is "against the wall," figuratively speaking. In other words you feel blocked. When you doubt belief is the key. When you have absolute belief in your abilities your back will stop bothering you. All of you know that you must eradicate your doubts of self-worth. Are the doubts getting you where you would like to be? Of course they are not. It's time for a little revision. Re-vision. Look again to your dreams. Look again to your actions. Look again to your behaviors.

I know that many of my creations have not been acting very lovingly. I take no joy in watching what I have created harming another creation. It matters not that the victim is man, plants, animals, or earth. I've had to watch all types of creations being harmed. However, I gave you free will. Each of you must take responsibility for your

145

actions. You must try to love yourselves. You must try to love or at least to tolerate each other.

You must try to love the planet where you live and to respect that which sustains that planet. You cut down trees. You destroy the rain forests. You ruin the land by littering and ravishing it. You muddy the waters with dirt and chemicals. You darken the air with pollution and make holes in the ozone layer. You still expect the planet to sustain you. I tell you this: you are going to have to make some behavioral changes if you want life to continue. You cannot live there if you cannot breathe. You must drink water and have food to survive. Yet you continue to destroy your life's necessities. You are beginning to live in a new millennium. Why not make the necessary changes that will enhance life rather than destroy it.

You see, but so many of you are so complacent about making changes. You call those people radicals whose concerns are such as I have spoken. Well, you need more such radicals. What can one person do? Write to your elected officials. Enact new laws that would prohibit damaging the environment. Yes, you have made a start with things like recycling. However, much more is needed.

Where would be the best place to begin? Begin within each one of you. Begin with yourself. Look at yourself. Really look at who you are at this very moment. What kind of person are you? Are you kind and loving to yourself as well as to others? Or are you hard as nails on yourself? Why should you love yourself any less than you love anyone else? When someone loves himself you call him selfish or egotistical. It is not selfish but self-love to nourish your own spirit.

Let others manage their own lives. Why must you need to control anyone else especially when you seem to have such a difficult time managing your own lives? Just stop and look at yourself first. Is your life what you would like it to be? What is really important to you? Why do you feel that it is important? Do you listen to what you say? Are your words kind and loving or do they condemn and hurt? Especially see what you do to yourself. What criticisms do you make of yourself and why? When are you being the person that your spirit truly is? Who is your true self? Why do you permit others to tell you how to feel about your self? Yet that is exactly what you to. You permit the opinions of others to influence how you feel about yourself. If someone else says that you are not beautiful because you are not in their image of beauty why do you accept their standards as your own? Your standards are just is valid as anyone else's. Who is to say they are right and you are wrong? Why do you not form your own opinions and hold fast to them?

Beauty is in the eyes of the beholder. That is the truth. Many times you look upon someone in disgust merely because they do not fit the image you prefer to look upon. You do not see the beautiful spirit who lies just beneath the exterior shell. You forget that I have fashioned each and every being after my own energetic image.

Listen to the thoughts you have. Are they loving or like venomous stings toward another? In this dimension spirits know that thoughts manifest immediately. Therefore, care is taken with thoughts. Where you dwell there is often a time lapse. Can you imagine what it would be like to have your thoughts realized instantly? They will, however, manifest eventually one way or another. Be careful of your thoughts.

I know. If you say that someone is the pain in the neck you can easily develop a stiff neck.

Exactly. More care must be taken about thoughts. Many articles are being written about the healing power of prayer. Is prayer naught but loving thoughts and petitions directed to me? I know that there are those of you who profess to hate me. I know that there are those of you who feel that I have forsaken or abandoned you. I know that there are those of you who do not believe in my existence. I know that there are those of you who feel unworthy to accept my love. No matter how hard you think I am on you, you are infinitely harder on yourselves. You may hide your thoughts and your feelings from one another and even from yourself but all is open to me. You can hide nothing from me. I know each of you better even than you know yourselves. I know how each of you truly feels about yourself, about all others, and about all things. With all of this knowledge I still love you—each and every one of you—all the saints and all the sinners, figuratively speaking. So the next time that you look into the mirror and see only supposed flaws, the next time another criticizes you or you criticize yourself, the next time you belittle yourself in any way, remember that you are my perfect and beautiful child.

You hold your fear related self-esteem issues in your middle back. You have let others whittle you down emotionally to the point of self-doubt. You doubt your opinions, your beliefs, your value, your self-worth, and for some of you, your very being. You are afraid to voice your opinions and beliefs because you feel that you will be ridiculed or belittled. You stifle your voice so as not to face confrontation. You are doing yourself a great disservice. Not only are you harming yourself emotionally you are allowing this harm to build within your body to the point of physical manifestation. Your opinion is just as valuable as that of anyone else. You have special gifts that are unique and yours alone. You are just as beautiful and special in my eyes as anyone else. Your life is valuable. So be proud of your individuality. You don't have to be perfect. If you are not happy with some aspect of your life then change it. If you can't change it learn to be content with the person you are. Stop being so critical of yourself and be more accepting. Play to your own strengths. Let your self-esteem and your middle back relax into the acceptance of who you are.

The middle back also incorporates the flip side of the heart chakra and all that implies. These are issues of self-love and issues of relationships. These, in fact, are any issues in relation to love; love of the job, love of a pet, or love of sports. These issues can manifest in the middle back when they are viewed in a negative light. It is when love issues become emotionally painful and that pain is not released that these issues express themselves physically. When there is a loss of the love of a person, pet, or object, does one not feel unsupported in some manner? When you're feeling unsupported isn't it logical that it would be displayed in the back? Is the spine not the support of the body?

How does one release the emotional pain associated with this area? Many people find it helpful to write a journal of their feelings. Other people find it helpful to take a picture of that person and place it upon a pillow or against a chair and speak to that person.

Many times unresolved issues block the energy in the back. Many people have feelings of guilt when they have lost a loved one before they were able to express all of their feelings. So often I hear, "I never got a chance to tell him that I love him." Don't you realize that just because the body is gone the soul can still hear across the dimensions? Talk to the picture. Call in the spirit of that person and they can hear what you say. Tell them all the things that you were never able to tell them while they were on the earth plane. Speak your truth from the heart. It is important to have closure and then to release any feelings of guilt or remorse. Carrying around these negative feelings only serves to build blockages in the energy field that will eventually manifest physically.

How long do you have to carry around grudges? How long do you have to carry around pain? How long must you feel vengeful when you feel a wrong has been done to you? The answer is simple. Deal with it and let it go. Those of you who have carried ill feelings towards another for ten, twenty, or thirty years are only hurting yourself. Let it go for the sake of your own physical well-being. Each time you think of that person in a negative manner you are sending him a portion of your own energy. Why do you fuel the negativity? Just let it go.

Those of you that have reached a higher spiritual level go one step farther. You ask that the person who has hurt you be surrounded and filled with extra light and love because you realize that by sending them love it will serve to heal them as well. By sending that person love you are healing yourself.

I would like to do a meditation with you that will help you to release the blockages in your back. Sit quietly in a place in which you know you will not be disturbed. Put on soft music if it will help you to relax. Take some deep breaths and slowly release them. Let your eyes gently close.

Picture my healing white-golden light gently flowing down from the heavens into the top of your head. Relax all of the muscles in your face and scalp while releasing any fears, any anxiety, or any stress of the day as the light gently flows down and fills your head. Let go of any tension as this beautiful light flows down your neck and shoulders, down your arms, and out of your hands. See the beautiful healing light gently flowing down and filling your entire torso as it relaxes your muscles. It flows down through your hips, down your legs, and out of your feet. Feel your body totally relaxed.

See yourself walking on a path of crushed white stones. Lovely little brightly colored wildflowers and flowering plants and trees line the sides of the path. It is a beautiful spring day. The temperature is perfect and you feel very comfortable as you walk along. The sky is a beautiful shade of blue. There may even be a fluffy white cloud lazily drifting overhead. You can feel the sunshine as it gently warms you. A soft breeze caresses your face. You are alone but you know that you are completely secure, completely protected, and completely serene. As you walk along you may hear birds singing or see little animals along your path.

Ahead of you is a lovely white marble building. Walk up the steps higher and higher until you come to large set of doors. They automatically swing open and you walk into the foyer of a magnificent white marble temple. The space you have entered is open to the sky. It is a round chamber with a series of doors around the perimeter. The sun is shining directly down on this area so that it is bathed in beautiful white light.

In the center of the chamber you see a large white marble platform with two chairs facing each other. You notice that one of the chairs is occupied. In the chair is that which you have lost: a loved one, a dear pet, or a job—whatever or whomever it is that is causing you pain. The job will be represented by a boss or a business associate. Walk up the stairs to the platform, and sit in the chair across from this person or being. He or it is as real to you as when you last saw him.

Talk to him. Say everything that is in your heart—things that you were perhaps not able to say when he was on the earth plane. Tell him you love him or tell him how much he hurt you. No one is there to criticize. No one is there to judge. It is just you and that other person or being. Tell him everything that you wanted to say to him but were unable to say. If you would cry, then cry. If you would yell, then yell. If you would hug him then lean over and hug him. Do not hold back any thoughts. Empty your heart of all the words and feelings. Pour out all of the love or all of the pain.

When you are completely spent, that person or being gives you a beautiful shining red heart which you place over your heart. You are keeping the love with you. If you are mourning the loss of the job, know that this heart that is being placed over yours is opening your heart to make room for some new ventures. You can release any sorrow or bitterness and look forward to wonderful new opportunities and challenges to come.

If you are dealing with the loss of a person or pet know that you take their love with you and that they will be around you. Talk to him and he will hear you. Give him a last goodbye and know that any time you wish to visit you may return to this beautiful marble temple and he will be here waiting to greet you.

Stand up and walk down the stairs, out the doors, and the down the long flight of stairs back to the beautiful path. As you walk along you feel energized and so much lighter and happier.

You return to your room and on the count of three bring yourself back to awareness. One, know you are sitting in your seat. Two, begin to feel the feelings in your body, your hands, your feet, and moving your neck. Three, open your eyes, smile, and become fully aware and awake.

If you find all sorts of aches and pains beginning to be felt within the body you have it within your power to heal all that you have created. Just take it one step at a time. Isolate where the dis-ease lies in your body. Really look at the underlying issues associated with that area. Deal with those issues. When the issues have been cleared visualize a healing taking place in that area. *Know* without a shadow of a doubt that you are healed.

I would just like to add a little bit more regarding this area of the back. Does it not make sense to see that you have been physically "putting your troubles behind you?" So why not do just that metaphorically? Let these hurts be "behind" you. Let them be in your past. You have all the support that you need if you will but fully let me into your life. Know that I support you in the manner that is for your highest good. If physical or emotional support is best I will send you physical or emotional help. If you have chosen the challenge to develop inner strength I support you always with love and will send you encouragement. If it is in your best interest to have angelic support then angelic support you will receive. Trust in me. Trust in yourself.

14

Those Boulders in My Shoulders

Today we will discuss the upper back. It is a most affected area. It is here that most people carry their burdens. Your expression is "shouldering the load." Problems that have manifested and multiplied and are held in the area of the shoulders and neck become seemingly solid. What feels like huge rocks within the muscles is the accumulation of tension. When concerns build over an extended period of time you believe that it would take an equal amount of time to resolve the issues. The reality is that it really doesn't have to take much time.

Let's begin with helping the physical aches for that is how the area will heal the fastest. What helps is to be relaxed with lots of deep muscle massage. Using a vibrator, hot oils, or going to a massage therapist is of great help. I would like to recommend being open to doing acupuncture also. Warm water baths or hot packs on that area ease the muscle tensions. Lift heavy items with leg muscles instead of back muscles. Stretch periodically. Try not to be so "stiff necked" with others. Deal with situations then let them go. Share or delegate perceived burdens.

This is all very basic information that we already know. Why should people buy a healing book to get this kind of information?

All of these remedies are well known but many are ignored. They will help to relieve aches of that area, but you must love yourself enough to do them. Men especially feel that self-pampering is a feminine thing to do. Following these remedies is being kind to your body.

Why do you feel only women can care for themselves? Men, you can still be and feel masculine and get massaged, too. You forget that I have created every human being with both masculine and feminine qualities. You need to balance your energies. You need to allow your nurturing qualities to make an appearance. It will make you a better man, a better father, a better husband, a better lover, and a much better human being. Begin by nurturing yourself.

Women, now I speak to you. Yes, you do nurture when it is appropriate. More often, however, it is nurturing others. Yes, today you are much better at self-pampering but act gentler to yourselves. You are so hard emotionally. If you look into the mirror and see some extra weight, a gray hair, or a wrinkle, you panic. Look into the mirror and look into your eyes. See who you truly are—not the physical image but the spirit beneath. That is truly the important image. A body will deteriorate no matter what cosmetic thing you do to it. Just accept that it will and rejuvenate the spirit instead.

The spirit is forever as young as it is desired to be. On the other side of the veil spirits choose to appear at any age they prefer. Here there is no age. There is no time. There is only eternity. Are you not in my image? Am I not eternal? I have no gender. I have no age. I have only love. Love. That is what I wish for you to have, too—love of me, love of yourselves, love of others, and love for my creations. If you cannot love then at least be tolerant of that which is different.

By examining the matters held in the shoulders and upper back we see that what is represented is the pain of shouldering guilt, shouldering responsibilities, and shouldering burdens or imaginary burdens. Let's deal with these issues. Guilt is the result of fear. There are basically only two emotions: fear, or its opposite which is love. Fear triggers guilt. Eliminate the underlying fear and you eliminate the guilt associated with that fear. "How do I do that?" is what you ask. It takes a bit of effort on your part because only you know what the underlying fear is. It requires some private time for you to sit down where you will not be disturbed and to really think about your life. Make a worksheet for yourself. By answering the following questions you will be able to release many old burdens and begin the healing process:

1. Where are you and what circumstances have brought you to this point?

2. Who were the people that had the greatest impact on your life either in a positive or a negative way?

3. Why are you still holding onto past hurts?

4. Why do you value other's opinions of you?

5. Whose opinions do you value?

6. Why is his or her opinion of you more important than your own opinion of yourself?

Keep in mind that I created everyone equally. Each spirit is just as important to me as any other. I love each one of you just as much as any other. Your thoughts are just as important and valuable as anyone else's. Another may have chosen a profession that appears to be more important or closer to me. In reality, though, it is not the profession but the spirit of the person doing that profession that is the most important.

I do not love the Pope any more than I love *you*. You are just as important to me. I realize that a statement like that may shock Catholics, but what is the Pope or any clergyman but another of my children. I created all of my children and I love all of you. Yes, I even love Hitler and the children who have not chosen a path of love and beauty. Each of you must find the loving path on your own. Until that time I will still love you. You are all part of me and deserving of all of my love, no matter how bad you think you have been, no matter what crimes you think you have committed. You will not go to hell. There is no hell but what you create in your own mind.

Lo, I have given unto you my love and it shall lift you out of the depths of what despair you have created. Yes, that is right. You have created whatever circumstances in which you find yourself. So stop blaming everyone else for your circumstances. Life happens *from* you. Life does not happen *to* you. I tell you yet again: on a soul level you chose what you wished to experience. The situations in which you find yourself were created to give you that experience. "But," you say, "I didn't choose to have cancer." Consciously, no, you didn't. However, you chose on a soul level to experience strength, faith, self-empowerment, or inspiration for others. So it was that you contracted cancer so that your spirit could experience whatever you chose. There are no accidents. Everything you do is for a reason. Stop feeling guilty about it. Look for the underlying reasons. Accept your own responsibility. Stop whining and complaining.

I hear everything—your prayers, your thoughts, and your innermost desires and secrets. You cannot hide anything from me. You only hide things from yourself and from others. Face what you are afraid of facing. Deal with it and let it go. Stop holding onto your guilt and fear. What good does it do to hold on? It does no good. It only builds itself until it begins to show in physical form. Stop punishing yourselves and hurting yourselves. It is so unnecessary.

If you feel you have wronged another apologize, make amends, or do whatever it takes to release your pain. If you feel you cannot face that person then write a letter to him. If he doesn't accept your apology it becomes his problem; it is no longer yours. You can release it. Even if that person has died you can still release it. Just because his body has died doesn't mean he can't hear you. His spirit is very much alive. Call him. Say what is in your heart. He will hear you. Know that I am with you and there is no reason to fear. Tell him what you were unable to say when he was on the earth plane. Say how much he hurt you; then forgive him. By not forgiving him you are only hurting yourself. It is you that hold anger or fear within your cellular structure.

Spirits will not or cannot harm you any more. Yes, they can make their presence known. However, you can protect yourselves. Do you not know that I will send help? You have but to ask and help will be sent. I have many masters on the earth plane and many angels who will help.

Sometimes you pray and it appears that I have not answered your prayers. I *always* hear your prayers, but there are times that your prayers are not in the best interests of either yourself or the person about whom you pray. Just because you wish something to be the way you would like does not mean that it is for the highest good. If you don't seem to receive the help you require, your highest good may be that you need to experience doing that job yourself. The conscious mind may feel that it's something you can't do alone, but your spirit knows what you have chosen to experience.

You pray for a dying loved one to recover. Only his spirit knows what is truly best for him. If it's not the time for him to leave help will be sent. However, if his spirit chooses to leave it's his choice and you must accept it. I know that that is particularly difficult for the parents of a child to accept. However, you must love enough to know that everything is in its correct time and place in the universe. I do not "take away" a loved one. It's always his choice to leave. I welcome him home to my loving arms figuratively speaking.

Now let's return to the shoulder and upper back area. Many of the burdens that you hold here are imaginary burdens. You picture yourselves like the wonderful mythological image of Atlas shouldering the burden of the world on his shoulders. What so many of you do is to hold your world on your shoulders. This is because when I designed the body I created strength in that area and it's the inner strength that is represented. Your inner strength reflects what you consider to be your responsibilities.

Let's work with what responsibilities you feel you must shoulder. You take on those responsibilities voluntarily. "But," you say, "I have a family to support." If it's the family have these responsibilities been chosen or just accepted? Must they be your responsibility alone or can they be shared? I know that many times you find yourselves in situations that seem to be hopeless, but you have chosen those situations whether or not you realize it. Of all the wishes you make to me, one of the most frequent ones is to ask for help with your challenges of responsibility. I hear pleas for finding a job or a home. Many are pleas for help with finding someone to lift some of the responsibilities from your shoulders.

Do you not realize what creations these are? By creating lack it forces you to not only experience that lack but also to accomplish the challenge of creation. It is you who create your life. It is you who create all of your situations by the choices that you make. There are always choices. Did you choose to have a spouse? Did you choose to have children?

What about the people who seem to get pregnant "by accident?"

I will say this yet again: there are no accidents. Everything happens for a reason and in its proper time.

God, could we please address the issue of abortion at this juncture?

Of course. As we have said, before you reincarnated you made agreements with other souls concerning your family situations. This includes the spirits that wished to come to you as your children. Although there were agreements there is still an element of free will that is in place. I know that there are situations when you feel that the time is not fortuitous to have a child.

Some of your more open-minded healers have begun a practice that serves both the child and assuages the conscience of the mother. They have the mother actually talk to the unborn child. She explains to him that it is not in the best interest of either the family or him that he should be born at this time. The mother can actually renegotiate with the child. In many cases this re-negotiation is sufficient to cause the child to naturally abort. If there is no abortion and the mother chooses to have the child she still has the choice whether to keep it and raise it or to permit it to be adopted.

The other option is her choice if she wishes to have a medical abortion. Again I tell you this: I do not judge. I do not punish. I will love all the parties concerned regardless of their choices.

What about the people who say that it is a sin and a murder to abort a child?

I repeat: I do not judge, I do not punish, and I will still love all the parties concerned. Let us address the people that talk of sin and murder. Let me first say that there really are no "sins" but those that are put into place by man. The religions invented sins to control the populace. I do not look as you look at the various acts that you tout as sins. I have a different perspective. Even you have different perspectives in your views of what is considered a sin.

Do you mean what the different cultures or even individuals consider as a sin? For example, many in some cultures do not consider it a sin to use their women and children as shields for the protection of their men because they do not place much value on their women. Even here in the West a robber or terrorist will use a human shield for self-protection. Those of us who consider physically harming another somewhat of a sin still harm others with emotional or mental abuse.

Those were very good examples. Everything depends on the perspective of the individual. Now with regard to murder, have you considered the larger picture? Are you not murdering yourselves every day? Is it not still suicide to kill your selves slowly? You are killing yourselves by ingesting harmful drugs, chemicals and alcohol. You are destroying your lungs by smoking and by breathing the air that you have polluted. You ingest the animals that you have treated with chemicals and pollutants that you have put into the water in which they live. You infect the ground waters that you ultimately drink. You destroy the rainforests and the ozone layer of your atmosphere that, in turn, destroys the air you breathe. You create more and more harmful viruses that become more resistant to immunization. Your collective consciousness creates diseases and weapons that annihilate a good portion of your population. Yet, if a person wishes to end his life quickly, painlessly, and with dignity, you punish those who try to assist him. If a person doesn't wish the responsibility to bring a child into the world you bomb the clinic and shoot the doctor who tries to assist her. Is that not committing murder as well? Some of those very people who cry "murder" of the unborn child, most of whom have not even had the soul enter the fetus at that juncture, are committing murder of adults.

I am sorry to observe that we are so quick to judge others but we are so blind when it comes to observing ourselves. We are so fortunate that you still love us in spite of ourselves. Thank you.

My sweet little teacher, there is nothing that any of you could do that would cause me not to love you.

I would like to continue addressing that which you consider the burdens that you shoulder. We mentioned earlier having the responsibility to support a spouse and children. A marriage should be a contract drawn with love between two people that are friends as well as lovers. It is not for one person to control the other. It is for two equal partners, each with his or her own likes and dislikes, talents, and challenges and each with an equal say in how their marriage will be conducted. Friends make requests of each other, not demands. Friends laugh together and cry together. Friends find joy in just being together.

Partners are friends that need to learn to communicate with each other without yelling, demanding, abuse or hysterics. A marriage shouldn't be a burden; it should be a pleasure. I know that people marry for numerous reasons. Some of you seem to have a need to feed off of each other. Don't you realize that this is a drain on your own energy as well? It is, of course, your free will to live in such a negative environment if that is what you choose, but I would suggest you rethink your situation. It is far healthier to live in a positive and loving environment.

Children can be wonderful, but they can also be a burden financially and emotionally. Are we opening a can of worms including children in this discussion?

Okay. Let's discuss children. Children can be a mixed blessing for many of you dependent upon your attitude. I created you to be creators. You create the situations of your life. You create your physical and emotional conditions. You have the ability to create a physical body for another soul to enter. It is your way of lovingly giving someone else the opportunity to return to the earth plane in order to speed up the progression of that soul back to the state of unconditional love and purity.

Yes, souls can have some experiences here in what you call heaven, but there are many things that can only be experienced in a physical body. So you create a child. How will your attitude affect that child? The soul of that child knows how things will be. What responsibilities you have toward that child are included in your pre-incarnation agreement with that soul. Many people ask how someone would choose to enter into a life of starvation, physical challenges, or abuse. It all depends on what that spirit wishes to experience. Keep in mind that there are always very good reasons for everything depending upon one's perspective. Therefore, I say to you, "Be not judgmental of another for you do not know his agenda." There are very good reasons for peoples' circumstances. Don't judge the homeless person, the person who lives in a third world country, or the king.

God, what if a soul is on the earth plane at the same time as the parents that he would choose? Then, he dies and chooses to reincarnate quickly. How can he make an agreement when the parties involved are already on the earth plane? I don't know if I stated that very clearly but you know what I mean.

I understand your question, and it is a very good question. The answer lies within the souls of the parties involved. When you sleep the physical body rests, but the spirit is always awake. In your dreams do you not fly occasionally? Do you not travel to places in your memory or to new places? Do you not see events that have already happened or that will come to happen in the future? Do you not have visitations with loved ones, many of whom have "died?" Are there not times when you dream that you are doing a physical exercise or sport during the night and you awaken feeling tired? As your body sleeps your soul leaves to work, to travel, or to visit.

No, you are not dead. Your soul is connected to your body by a long silver cord and may return instantly whenever it desires. Your body was designed to continue its functions of breathing, pumping blood to your heart, and so forth without any effort on your part and does so while your soul is free to come "home." In order for your soul to have the experiences that it desires in a body it must slow its vibrations to match the denseness of a physical body. That can feel like a burden to a soul. So the soul may experience freedom from the body when the body sleeps. That is one reason why some people feel that they require more sleep than others. That spirit wishes to have less time in the physical body.

Many of you have been able to allow the soul to "astral travel" while you are in a meditative state. For most of you this is achieved while you sleep. When your soul is not hampered by your physical awareness it may visit with other energies, entities, or souls of those who are on the earth plane. This is how agreements may be reached even after some of those spirits have reincarnated.

I would like to end this chapter by saying that burdens are only burdens by your perception. Circumstances that appear as burdens can be viewed completely differently with a different perspective. If you are not content with your situation, look to see where changes are to be made. This may require a change in your attitude rather than your physical circumstances. Can't you share your perceived responsibilities?

If you are single, what changes can you make to lighten your load? Remember that there is a law of attraction in place. What vibrations are you sending out into the world? What are your beliefs? Do you whole-heartedly believe that you can improve your situation? Have you still not realized that for every circumstance there is a reason? You *can* meet your challenges. You *can* create a new situation and change your life. *Know* that you can. Trust in me and trust in yourself. Believe.

15

Healthy Hands

I am going to write about an area that is somewhat complex—the hand. Must people be so careless with what is very delicate? I created hands with a very intricate structure because of their function. It's the hands that not only physically hold but also represent being able to hold. The fingers, which I will discuss individually, represent the little details of life.

Is there a difference between the left hand and the right hand?

Yes there is. Usually the left side of the body is representative of feminine issues and the right side of masculine issues. This is not to say that if you are female and your right hand hurts that there is a male in your life who is hurting you. That could be, but more likely than not it is masculine issues which trouble you.

Masculine issues involve strength. Dear ones, strength is the inner strength of character, the strength to live your life with honesty, trust, integrity, and love.

Feminine issues involve softness, gentleness, and nurturing. What better gifts are there to your self as well as to others? A difficult challenge for so many is to be loving and gentle to your self. Most find it easier to love others, but you are so hard on yourselves. Each being was created with a balance of both feminine and masculine qualities and it is important to find and to maintain that balance.

I would like to clarify that hand situations usually represent minor issues. I am not saying that the hand injuries or conditions are minor. What I am saying is that the fingers are the extremities of the body. The little issues that are represented here are sometimes put aside rather than dealt with because they are at the extremities of your life. Many times people neglect the small issues because they are so busy dealing with major issues. This is understandable. If there are many of these issues and if they have been piling up for a long time, they will eventually display themselves physically.

The Little Finger

Let's begin with the little finger. When the little finger is damaged look into what balances your life. The brain is more balanced when both halves are exercised. Like anything else the more it is used the better it remains. Creative right-brained people need to exercise their left-brain skills. Instead of using a calculator do math by long hand. Solve mental puzzles. Logical left-brained people need to use their imaginations. Be creative. Use your artistic abilities and life will be much calmer and so much better.

An indicator of unbalance is when you repeatedly injure your little finger. Look to see where your life balance has shifted. It could be an indication that you have been neglecting part of your brain. Perhaps the unbalance is a reflection of your family life or relationships. Make the time to look at your life. Are you being honest or are you pretending? Are you working and neglecting your relationships? Are you completely tied up with family and neglecting your own spiritual growth? Little fingers will tell you to check. Maybe the changes will be the little kind. Maybe not, but notice how you injure yourself. Are you doing small injuries or breaking bones? It demonstrates how your life is being reflected.

The Ring Finger

Next is the ring finger. Do you notice that this is the finger that is generally the weakest digit? That is because unless you are a hermit living alone on an island or have locked yourself away in your home you must deal with people every day. This finger involves the little annoyances that people have with regard to family and relationships. Most people who have a very good relationship with their spouse or in today's vernacular, significant other, have a tendency to forget that there are many types of relationships. There are those of a partner, parent and child, sibling, you and co-workers or friends, committee members, teacher and child, or doctor and patient. More of these relationships are the cause of difficulties and challenges. People sometimes bury these little upsets by pretending that everything is fine. Eventually they will build to a crescendo and erupt on the surface one way or another.

The answer is communication. Every action, every conversation, and every confrontation has the potential to change your life or to change the life of the person with whom you are speaking. You can make a difference. You have numerous thoughts. You use numerous words every minute. Are they positive or negative? Are they hurtful or helpful? You can change your thoughts and words if you really wish to change lives. Listen to what comes out of your mouth. Pay attention to the thoughts in your head. Be the person you wish to be. Strengthen your relationship with humanity.

Instead of pretending and hiding why not gently mention your thoughts to whoever is annoying you? You don't have to yell, to make demands, or to attack. Just speak quietly and let the other person know that you feel upset. You could suggest how the situation might be changed so as not to be hurtful. Are you afraid to speak to that other person? If so, why are you afraid? Why are you still living in a fearful situation? Is your self-esteem so low that you continually allow yourself to be abused?

I know that we have gotten away from minor disturbances that are represented in the ring finger and are moving into a major issue that can be found manifested in other parts of the body. I must tell you this: you are a worthwhile person. You are just as precious, just as valuable, and just as important as the one whom you are allowing to abuse you or to control you. Find your inner strength either to speak with that other person or to leave that situation. It is still your choice as to whether you will allow yourself to be abused or used either physically or verbally.

There is another relationship or two that also can present challenges—you with yourself and you with God. If the fourth finger is ailing look to which relationship may be hurting or weak. Strengthen your relationship with yourself. Strengthen your relationship with God.

<u>The Middle Finger</u>

The middle finger will indicate both strength and loving. This is physical strength or how your body feels that is being manifested. There may be a physical deficiency that needs attention. This is when it is important to communicate with your body. Your body will tell you what it is lacking. It will show you a picture of a food that contains that which you lack or you will see a sentence or word in your mind's eye. You may even hear the words. The important thing is that you listen to your body. When your body wishes to have spinach because it lacks iron make it your priority to eat spinach.

An addendum to physical strength is your attitude toward your body. Are you angry with your body? The middle finger can also hold anger. Try not to see what you consider the imperfections of your body. Instead, concentrate on all of the wonderful functions that your body performs.

When you have a middle finger injury it would behoove you to have a willingness to change. Sometimes change requires great inner strength. It is not easy to be outside of your comfort zone. At times the change needed will take a complete turn around in attitude. Links between old habits and new ones must be broken, but it is up to you to decide how important it is to do what ever it is that you need to do. Becoming aware must be the first step in the process. You must step back and take a good look at the person you are. Then, if this is not the person you would like to be, what changes will be necessary for you to become that person? Now that you see your wishful self do the following: make a list of the attributes you would like to have. In another column list your personality characteristics that you would like to release.

How do you proceed in bringing to fruition this list? Take one item at a time and really concentrate on that item for as long as it takes to change. For example, you have decided that you would like to be less controlling. Watch yourself very carefully. Who is it that you have made a habit to control? Is it a spouse, a child, or a co-worker? When you begin to see yourself in that position, stop and breathe. Close your mouth. You are doing a great disservice to them as well as to yourself. They may not be doing things the way you would do them or the way you would like them to be done, but it is time for you to let go. Unless their decision and choice is *directly* affecting your life, stay out of it. Don't give an opinion unless they ask for it. You do them a disservice by manipulating the situation. How are they to follow their agenda if you do not allow them the freedom to make their own choices and decisions? Why are you preventing their growth? Don't you see this as selfish?

Suppose you wish to change the way in which you accept others controlling you. Why do you permit another to make decisions for you? Do you still not realize that you are there for your own soul's progression? Is it not time for you to take charge of your own life? Is fear so intense that it prevents you from change? It's up to you to choose how you will live.

Have you noticed that this is the finger people use when showing their anger?

Yes, there is anger displayed with this finger. Keep in mind, however, that fingers represent minor angers. Isn't that display demonstrated as a spur of the moment show of anger or disgust? It isn't a highly evolved being that uses such displays. A highly evolved being would not consider hurting the feelings of another by such a gesture. If you are reading this book it is an indication that you are making a conscious effort to advance your spiritual growth.

Perhaps you must learn to control your anger and your temper. It takes much self-control to hold back rage. Teach yourself control. There must be a concerted effort to change. Breathe. Make an effort to take deep breaths in through your nose. Concentrate on filling your whole body with oxygen. Exhale slowly through your mouth. If you must leave the room to avoid screaming at another, then leave. Do yourself the favor of learning to calm your self. You will be healthier for it. Find your inner strength. Learn to release your anger privately. If need be take a class in anger management.

I created each and every one of you with all of the facilities you need. I know that some of you will argue that there are those who are mentally or physically handicapped. Again I say to you that I have created each and every soul with the facilities that they need. When a person comes into this life with a supposed handicap or acquires one during their lifetime it's because that's the path that they have chosen in order to experience that which they have deliberately chosen to experience. Yes, be empathetic, be helpful, but love enough to let them have their experience. Let them gain their independence or inner strength to the level that they can. You don't know what their agenda contains. Do you wish for them to need another similar lifetime because they have not had their experience?

Don't judge. You don't walk in another's shoes. You don't know what has brought another to his present situation. You don't know what his soul planned to experience. Look not at another with condemnation, but look lovingly with an open heart. Again you ask about murderers and abusers. I repeat to you: judge not for you do not know of their souls' missions. Perhaps it was the choice of the victim to experience being a victim because at some former life he had been a murderer. In essence, it's a very loving thing for a soul to make an agreement before entering the earth plane to give another his experience. Here all is love. It's a sacrifice to step away from all encompassing love.

Aren't we digressing from the topic a bit?

Not really. We were talking of how the middle finger indicates strength and love. So love yourself enough to look inward and to make those changes that will be beneficial. Love others enough to let them change their world. You can really only change yourself. By changing yourself it changes the world around you. Remember that life truly happens from you. Your soul always has a reason for everything even if your conscious mind knows it not.

Learn to trust. Trust in me that I hear your prayers and your thoughts, and I know your feelings always. Sometimes I send help when help is truly needed, but sometimes I love you enough to let you have the experience of meeting your challenge by yourself. I tell you yet again: I *always* love you. I send encouragement. I send signs. Always your prayers are answered in one way or another. The answers may be very subtle. I put them in front of you, but so many times you ignore them or refuse to see them. What a feeling of accomplishment is yours when a challenge is well met by your own strength and by your own accomplishment. Isn't that worth the sometimes very difficult work required?

The Index Finger

Let's continue by discussing the index finger that also denotes strength. When you have injured this finger look to see where you are losing your strength. What kind of strength have you been losing? Is it physical strength? Where has it manifested in the body? Look to your energy centers to help you determine the issues related to this loss. There are very valid books in the market that clearly describe the chakra energy centers and the issues related to each center. I ask you to read a book that goes into detail on this subject.

I think that Caroline Myss gives wonderful information on the charkas in her books.

I agree. Let's continue.

There are many different types of strength. There is strength of character. Do you stand up for your beliefs and principles? Are you being honest with yourself and others? Do you let others belittle and criticize you for your beliefs?

There is strength of conviction. Are you taking charge and responsibility for your own life or are you letting others do this for you? Are you taking the easy way out or are you working through your challenges with grace, dignity, and tenaciousness? Are you completing your tasks and challenges or giving up because they are difficult?

There is spiritual strength. Do you question your connection with me? Do you blame me for a loss or for the situation in which you find yourself? So many times I have heard you pray to me with bargains and deals if only I would help. When your loved one dies or the situation doesn't go as you would have hoped you blame me, you lose faith in me, or you abdicate your responsibilities and leave everything in my hands. Yes, I will send help when it is appropriate to do so. However, there are times when it is in your best interest to do a thing yourself. I will always do what is in your best interest, whether or not you know or you think you know what that is. It takes strength of will to keep your faith and belief in the face of frustration or pain. Have faith in me, but also have faith in yourselves and your own strengths and abilities. I have instilled in each of you strengths, gifts, and abilities. Find them within yourselves and use them in love.

Keep in mind, too, that this is your index or "pointing" finger. At whom are you pointing a finger? Why are you being so judgmental? You don't walk in another's shoes. You don't know the blueprint that he has drawn for this life. You don't know the challenges that he has faced that have brought him to this point in time. You don't know the agreements that he made with others prior to his incarnation. Do you not have enough problems and challenges in dealing with your own life without presuming to criticize another? As Shakespeare wrote: "To thine own self be true." Let each live his own life according to his own plans without your interference.

People are going to ask about when we see abuse and terrorism. Are we just to stand by and watch while innocent people are being hurt?

Of course not. If there is a situation in which injury can be prevented and the abused is willing to accept help, then help. Keep in mind that there are very good reasons why those people are in that situation. Both the abuser and the victim have very good reasons for being where they are. Ultimately, however, it is their own agendas and it is not your place to do their clearing for them. This is not to say that you cannot be of help. It is their choice and free will to heal in love or to retain their fears. Make no mistake. Both the abuser and the victim are acting out of fears. If you are in a position to help them to heal and they are open to receiving help, then by all means help.

I would like to continue discussing the index finger. Do you not notice that when you point at another there are three fingers pointing back at you? If you are pointing at yourself why are you being so hard on yourself? You don't have to be perfect. That is my job. How is your self-esteem? Where does your fear lie? Are you over-compensating with your ego? Do you feel that what you have is not enough? Do you not know yet that there is always enough of everything and it is always available to you? Whatever you wish to draw to you, give that thing away. If it is health, help others to heal. If it is wealth, be generous with what you have. If it is peace, help others to find peace.

Do you feel that the person you are is insufficient in some manner? You still don't grasp the perfection of your own being if you should feel thusly. I created you as a reflection of myself. Am I not perfect? Your bodies are miracles in themselves. Your spirits are miracles within and around those bodies. You each have such potential that few of you have realized even half of that potential. Each of you has the ability to heal yourself and help others to heal should you so choose. Each of you has the ability to rise to tremendous heights, to create miracles of your own choosing, and to be the divine creature you truly are. The only one holding you down is you.

There is also an element of fear related to this finger. When you shake this finger at another to scold them what is the message that you give? Are you actually telling them that your opinion is more important? Is it one of the ways that you show your control over them? Are you trying to make them feel ashamed or guilty? Does this make you feel more important? Is it really teaching a child to be a more responsible person by belittling him? What is the underlying fear? Are you just emulating your parents without thinking your own thoughts? The next time you point or shake your index finger at another stop and consider why you do this.

The Thumb

Now I would like to discuss the thumb. Here we have the most expressive of the digits. It's the thumb that has the ability to grasp. It's the thumb that holds, but what it holds can be quite indicative of a number of areas. Physically, it is self-explanatory. What it truly indicates is holding onto life, holding onto your ideals, holding onto love issues, or holding onto your beliefs. If you find that you have created soreness or injury to your thumb ask yourself what it is that you are not grasping or what it is that you are trying not to hold.

Let's look at the individual areas of interest indicated by thumb injuries. To figure out what it is you are not grasping or trying to release, look at the issues involved throughout the chakra system. In which area does your worry lie? Relax, close your eyes, and begin going through each energy center while asking yourself to look at what is involved in that area at the time.

Begin with the base or root chakra. What is happening with your family, friends, job, religion, or any other tribal organization in which you are a participant? What is it that you are trying so hard not to hold on to? What concepts are you not grasping or willing to no longer hold? Who or what do you truly feel you must release? Something or someone is making you sore or causing you pain. Look to your groups to see what is amiss. Are you questioning religious issues? Have you been in conflict with your family?

If you feel that everything is satisfactory in that area move up to the second chakra. How are your personal relationships? Is your creativity being stifled? Have you been worrying about your finances? Are there sexual conflicts? Have you been experiencing physical discomfort in this area of the body? What or who are you reluctant to release? What or who are you having difficulty holding on to? Why? Search your true feelings.

Continue up the body through each energy center by asking yourself questions. See if you have been experiencing other physical manifestations in any of these areas. Soreness or pain is not a bad thing. It is an indicator of things to explore within your self. It is all right to take an aspirin or medication to help alleviate the pain, but don't forget to examine its origin. Medication does not solve why the pain occurred. Science can show you why the physical manifestations occur, but why have you created the underlying condition?

I know that some of you will argue that you have a physical propensity toward a particular condition because of your family genetics. That seems an easy explanation, but the answers are actually more complex.

<u>First</u>, you chose the body into which you incarnated. You chose your parents, your circumstances, and your physical condition in your blueprint. This includes the genes that you inherited. If there were physical conditions that might help you to have your desired experience you may have chosen a body that would afford you the opportunity to have those experiences.

<u>Second</u>, just because your body may have the capability to have a physical condition doesn't mean that you have to have it. In other words, just because every other member of your family has cancer doesn't mean that you have to have cancer. If it's not in your agenda then you will not have cancer. Conversely, if your soul feels that it would be in your best interest you can have cancer even if you are the only member of your family to do so. Of course I am not just referring to cancer but to any condition.

<u>Third</u>, you may develop a condition as a help to others as Christopher Reeve and many others have done. I discuss this in another chapter.

Thumb injuries are indications of deeper fears than are represented in the other digits. Most times what you fear and worry about exists only in your imagination. Little fears look larger when they are replayed repeatedly. Wouldn't it be easier to deal with each little fear before it becomes magnified? Pay attention to what your body tells you. Do you feel little butterflies in your stomach? Is there panic rising in your throat? Are your hands beginning to shake or to perspire? If you begin to feel physical symptoms of fear, stop. Breathe. What is the real fear?

For example, if you must speak in public what is it that you really fear? Is it criticism or judgment? Are you not thoroughly prepared? Do you question your own capabilities or worth? Get a grasp of the situation. As it has been said many times before, "feel the fear and do it anyway." You *can* overcome your challenges. You will find that fear is only False Evidence Appearing Real.

What does it indicate if you sprain your hand or wrist?

Sprained Muscles

Sprained muscles are an indication of a temporary reluctance to grasp something in your immediate future. It's really just a fear coming to the surface. Why are you hesitant to grasp what you perceive is coming? How will your life change? People have a tendency to first see the negative when faced with the unknown. Instead of feeling fear, try to capture the feeling of excitement. Look at your impending change as a new adventure that will bring golden opportunities and expansion.

Carpal Tunnel

I would like to add a little about conditions of the hand such as carpal tunnel and soreness brought on by repeated actions. Not everything has a deeper meaning—unless it does. Act responsibly. If you are doing an activity repeatedly, be smart. Take breaks. Rest your hands. Change positions. Stretch your muscles frequently. Be more thoughtful of your hands. Don't wait until you have diminished their capabilities to appreciate them. Hands hold and release. Hands soothe. Hands help you create. Hands express your feelings. Love your hands because, symbolically, you hold your world in your hands.

16

Head Toward Healing

<u>The Scalp</u>

Today I will speak to you about irritations that occur in the area of the head and throat. Let's begin with the scalp. At the top of the head lies the energy center known as the "crown chakra." It is through this center that the vibrations most easily enter and exit the body. This is the area where your conscious mind connects with your spirit and the spiritual aspects of life. Your spirit is actually all around you and through you, but your best connection is where it hovers over your head.

When you have sensitivity or an injury in the area of the scalp it is an indication that you are feeling separated from your spiritual side. Many of you feel very spiritual about your connection with me but you are still feeling separateness between us. You still don't accept that you and I are one. You don't accept the Godliness of your own soul. You still don't accept the perfection and the beauty of the person you really are—my perfection. Forgive yourself for your own imagined imperfections and for what you feel you are lacking. No matter what you have done or think you have done I still love you. It's never too late to change. It's never too late to remember who you really are. It's never too late to grow. It's never too late to become enlightened. Lighten up; stop being so hard on yourselves. I forgive you. Now forgive yourselves.

When I speak of improvement I am not referring to physical attributes. I am referring to inner qualities. The body is a temporary and changeable creation. It's already perfect in its functions and attributes. I'm more interested at this juncture in the evolution of your soul. Let's move on.

<u>Sinus Irritations</u>

There are a great many of you that complain of sinus irritations and inflammations. There are separate areas of pressure that I wish to discuss. Let's begin with the area in the center of the forehead just between the eyebrows.

The forehead center is the area just below and encompassed by the "third eye." When a blockage occurs in this area examine your dreams, or lack thereof. I am not referring to the dreams that you have during your sleeping hours. I am referring to the dreams you have for your life. What goals have you set for yourself? Have you lost track of those dreams?

So many times you tell me that you feel lost and you don't know which path to take. I tell you this: you are always on the "right" path. There are no accidents. There are no wrong turns because each turn that you have taken has led you to the point at which you are now standing. Your soul yearns for any and all experiences whether they are pleasant or challenging because no matter what the experience to truly know it is to experience it's opposite. If you are now questioning the direction for your future you must remember that this is just a choice of preference. All experiences will be ultimately beneficial.

Where would you like to be at this time next year? Are you content doing what you are presently doing? Are you happy with your present situation? Is this where you would like to be in five years from now? If your answer is yes, then continue along these lines until you are no longer satisfied and desire a change. If your answer is no, where does your discontentment lie? Is it in your relationships? Is it your working situation? Are you not content and at peace within yourself? If you are unhappy, what is it that is making you so unhappy?

Look at your present situation. If you are unhappy with the choices that you have made that led you to your present condition you have the free will to change your situation. You must decide if you really wish for a change. What will happen to your life if you make the changes needed to make you happy and at peace? Most people stay in conditions that make them miserable because they are afraid.

In Western cultures people let monetary circumstances hold them back. It can be frightening to quit your job and to find another. Sometimes you have stayed in that position so long that now you feel you cannot find another job because of your age. Society's emphasis on youth has made this a real concern for many middle-aged people. Those who have reached an age when retirement is strongly suggested are at a loss when they must make real life changes. This is what your society has mandated and unless the consciousness of the larger group is awakened changes will not occur. It is up to the collective mind to take into consideration the entire population and its needs. It is the collective thought that influences what has become the norm in business attitude.

I understand what you're saying. I know that it is up to each of us to change the thoughts of the collective consciousness. However, we who are working toward enlightenment seem to be in the minority. How can we help?

I know that it appears that the world is falling apart. I know that the media has placed an emphasis on younger generations and their supposed needs. I know that money has become the foremost concern of your societies. The slogan of so many of you has become "bigger is better." You strive for bigger homes, better furnishings, more expensive cars, and luxury vacations. It generally takes two people to maintain that lifestyle or one who excels in sports, acting, or business. At what cost are these goals? Is it benefiting your children? Is it making you a better person? I understand your desire for a life of luxury. Is it a life of ease? Is it a life of neglect of those you love? Are you harming yourselves with the easy availability of chemical substances? I am not saying that you cannot have this lifestyle. I am merely observing some of the ramifications. It is up to you to choose what is important. I observe that your monetary system does seem somewhat unbalanced. It is up to you to look past your own gratification and to balance the whole. It is up to each of you do choose your thoughts and actions. That is how the collective consciousness will change.

Speaking of monetary circumstances many of you stay in relationships because of financial concerns. What would your life be like if you were single and had to get a job or to change jobs? If there were jobs available in which you are interested would it create a hardship to accept a lesser paycheck? If it required you to move to another location what would be holding you back from moving? If there are young children or other loved ones that you don't wish to leave what changes could you make that would bring you contentment? You have made the choices that have brought you to your present state, and you must make the choices that will bring you inner peace. I will not tell you what to do. You must choose for yourselves.

Some Eastern and third world cultures play by a whole other set of rules. People there are not always at a mind to change their own lifestyles or to make independent decisions about their outer world. They have chosen to experience what life is like without such freedom of choice. I am not judging them, nor should you. For in truth, it is a beneficial experience for many souls. For spirits who have lived lives where they controlled others it is a grand experience for them to know how it feels to be on the receiving end. When they "die" they will feel richer for having had the experience.

I thought we all had free choice. Can they not leave home? Can they not emigrate to another country?

Yes, these things are possible. For most, however, they are not viable options. They have pre-chosen the circumstances into which they were born for particular reasons. The cultures in which they incarnated have determined sets of man-made rules by which they choose to live. You are thinking inside the box of Western civilization. Try to step into the thinking of other cultures to broaden your horizons. One way is not better than another given the circumstances and mentality of the collective consciousness of each area. Everything is relative.

Let's continue to the sinus cavities beneath the eyes.

The sinus cavities beneath the eyes are directly in the front of the face. Doesn't that tell you that there are things that you don't wish to "face?" What have you been avoiding? Why are you frightened? What is the worst thing that could happen to you if you wholeheartedly faced whatever you have been avoiding? Do these sinus cavities hurt in addition to the upper cavities? Are you afraid to face your future? Are you afraid to face having your dreams?

I want to say a few words about facing your inner self.

First, I know that many of you fear looking inward because you are afraid of whom you truly are. Some of you fear that you are such a terrible person that either I could never love you because you have done what you consider to be terrible things, or that you are lacking in some areas, or even that you are empty inside. All of that is rubbish. It is only your fear that is stopping you. Remember that I love every single one of my creations no matter what. Yes, I even love Hitler.

For those whom you have just upset by that statement would you please add some clarifying words?

Yes. I created all of you. You chose the type of person you are with the free will that I gave you. Nothing you could possibly do could take away my love for you. I will just quickly reiterate that it was the collective consciousness that created a Hitler. As an individual he never could have made possible the events that transpired. No, he had the approval and the cooperation of millions. It was not until the demise of millions of Jews and others that the collective consciousness became aware and awakened enough to stop those activities.

It is observable that people become involved when things become personal. The United States became involved in World War II for a number of reasons. Had they been strictly humanitarian reasons you would have intervened much earlier than you did. If the collective concern of the world had cared for their fellow human beings the outcome of the war would have been different. There were many countries that did not become involved. There were influential religious and political leaders that did not become involved. Much of the world closed its eyes to the atrocities happening in Europe and Japan. Ask yourself why this is so.

Why do you close your eyes and ears when you see a neighbor being attacked? You say that you don't wish to get involved. Look at the world today. Is it not still evident that you usually get involved only when things become personal? Can you not help your brother who is struggling or being attacked because he is your brother? It seems to be politics, economics, or personal assault that determines when you get involved. This is not a book on politics so let's return to our original dialogue.

Second, none of you are lacking anything. You each have been given all the tools and gifts that you require. Stop comparing yourselves with the next person. Each of you is unique and special unto yourself. Instead of trying to measure up to anyone else, be the best that you can be.

Third, some of you are afraid that you are empty inside. That is utter nonsense. Look back at your life at all the things that you have accomplished and all the people that you have touched. You keep forgetting that you are a part of me. I am the all. I am the alpha and the omega. I am all-powerful and complex. How can you, being part of me, be any less? Your bodies alone are incredible creations. Your minds are so complex that you do not know the half of their capabilities. Being special has nothing to do with having money or power. Play to your individual strengths. Don't be afraid to really see the beautiful spirit that you are.

God, may I please interject something?

Of course.

Here we are talking about healing the sinus. I must admit that I am the first one to take a pill. That hides the symptoms but they do re-occur peri-

odically. I do try to find the answers within myself but I seem to have some difficulty in completely healing myself.

You are a good example of many that are walking the path of self-improvement and enlightenment. You are pretty good at delving into the underlying issues, but you do not take it to the full extent. I would suggest that you continue to delve even deeper. You still carry some of your fears. You know about releasing them intellectually, but your emotional self still holds onto those doubts and fears. You also know that for you meditating on a more regular basis is the key to unlocking many of your challenges. Do you notice how often you block yourself by making yourself "too tired?" I am not chastising you. I am merely pointing out the obvious. If you choose to slow your progression, that's fine with me. Anything that you do is fine with me. However, if you wish to speed things up do what you know you need to do and stop procrastinating.

The Eyes

Let's proceed by discussing the eyes. Just what is it that you don't wish to see? When there are issues that you are avoiding you create conditions within the eyes such as blurring or tearing as avoidance mechanisms. This is different than not facing issues. In this situation you are really in denial. Never mind not wishing to deal with certain issues. You rebel against even knowing what the issues are. Blurring the eyesight is an indication that you are diffusing issues so as not to have to see them clearly. Do you not have an expression about not seeing something that is right in front of your nose? You cannot see it if you are not willing to open your eyes.

I understand about adults needing glasses, but what about children who need glasses? They have not been here long enough to create issues. What about people that are born blind or become blind?

Okay, I see that I will have to back-up. Many times when children require glasses it's because they don't wish to "see" things that are occurring in their present family situations. Even babies are aware of their environment.

There may also be another possibility. Do you not remember that each soul has been around since the creation? Babies are not new souls. Only the bodies are new. Each soul carries within him memories of every past life, every thought, every word, and every action. These memories are recorded and locked away so that they will not hamper this new adventure. However, if necessary, they can be accessed through the subconscious. Do you not think that over many lifetimes you have not acquired issues that you have neglected to remedy? You can carry into your present lifetime old wounds, hurts, or angers that you have not released. These old issues may even appear in the form of physical manifestations.

I understand that. I have always felt that I carried over a reduced breathing capacity this lifetime from a past life

That's a good example. Your lungs are physically capable of sufficient breath. The deficiency results from an emotional carry over. You know that and have been working it out. There is also the blueprint that souls make before incarnating into their present lives. It is for each to decide what it is that they wish to experience. If a person has chosen blindness there are a number of things that they could have desired to experience. How many of you are walking around as blind with your eyes wide open? You can be very creative in your avoidance.

The Throat and the Jaw

Let's continue moving down the face to the throat and the jaw. I think that it's pretty obvious that if you have created "lock jaw," TMJ, or any condition in which you clench the jaw, have a sore throat, or have created a condition that prevents you from speaking that you are trying to hold back your words. Are you clenching to hold back anger or resentment? What is it that you are trying so hard not to say? Are you stifling the creativity of your words? What is it that you are afraid to communicate? Why is it so difficult for you to speak your truth?

"May the words of my mouth and the meditations of my heart be acceptable unto You, Lord," people pray. Do you not realize, my dear children, that everything is acceptable unto me given my perspective? When you hold back your words you are not damaging me, for in truth, you cannot damage me in any way.

You are damaging yourselves. If you hold in your words for long enough those thoughts and feelings will continue to build and begin to "eat away" at your physical body. I'm not telling you to go out and hurt others with your words. You can speak your truth to others with loving words and gentle tones. You can speak your truth to yourself with loving words and gentle tones. If you feel that you cannot speak your words directly to another at least release the anger within yourself. (Releasing anger is discussed in more detail in the chapter on letting go of physical and emotional bonds.) Fear not for I am always—all ways, with you. Some of your words may be unpopular with the unaware masses. You may receive criticism. You may receive condemnation. You may also receive praise and encouragement. Go on take the leap of faith—faith in me and faith in yourself and your own convictions. Speak your truth lovingly. My love, you know what is Truth with a capital "T."

What about people who clench their jaws or grind their teeth while they sleep?

That is a sign that they are not releasing the daily tensions of their waking hours.

The Teeth and Gums

Some of you are so fearful of making changes or demonstrating that you are an independent thinker that you create teeth or gum damage. You are afraid to "take a bite" out of life. I realize that sometimes it is easier to let others make decisions for you. I know that for some of you your challenge this lifetime is just making decisions. You are so fearful of the opinions of others that you continually hesitate to choose in case you should look foolish. Why is their opinion better than yours? Why are their selections better than yours? I created everyone with similar capabilities. Your opinions and selections are just as important as those of anyone else. You are just as worthy, just as important, and just as lovable as anyone else.

So many decisions that you hesitate to make are so minor. Is it the blue one or the red one? Stop being wishy-washy; just choose one. If it makes you unhappy you can always change it later. Most of your decisions are not those of life or death. Be brave. Trust in yourself. Trust in your own intuition. Trust in your own self-worth. Trust that your decisions are of value. In truth, they are of immense value in the overall scope of your life. Just the act of stepping out of your comfort zone and making decisions is a leap of progress. Take a big bite out of life. You chose to be here at this time. Relish that choice. Roll up your sleeves and jump in with both feet. Enjoy your time there. Breathe the air, smell the flowers, hug a cat, love a friend, and make decisions with conviction and confidence.

Hearing Challenges

If you are having discomfort or have created a hearing deficiency or tinnitus ask yourself these questions: What is it that I am avoiding hearing? To what or to whom do I not wish to listen? The issues here can result from a stubbornness to be willing to listen not only to others but also, possibly, to your own inner voice. It is important to listen to that "still small voice within." Learn to trust your own intuition. It knows what is in your best interests. If you get a good or bad feeling about something don't ignore that feeling. It is a valid indication that your soul is trying to talk to you.

How are you consciously talking to yourself? To which voice are you listening? Do you find it easier to listen to the negative voices that play and replay in your mind? Are you listening to the voices of your parents, teachers, or peers when they have denigrated you? What makes their opinions more important than your own? Are you listening to your own voice being negative and telling you that you have physical or mental deficiencies? If all you are hearing are the negative thoughts then it is very understandable that your soul has created a self-protection and preservation of blocking out that which you hear. Stop listening to and creating the negative, right now. Every time you hear a negative thought, stop and cancel that. Turn it around into something positive. You can do it! Start hearing your own inner voice that tells you that you are loved, that you are perfect just as you are, that you are worthy, and that you have talent.

Deafness

What about people who are born deaf?

There are many reasons why a person should choose to enter a life in silence. Perhaps in a past life they caused the deafness of another and wished to experience the result of their actions to that other. Perhaps they were very controlled and now wished to have the strength to have to listen to their own convictions, to their own voice. Perhaps they lived a life filled with noise, yelling, or cacophony and wished for silence. Perhaps they came as a loving gesture to help those who have hearing deficiencies and felt that they would be more understanding if they could experience that condition. Could not people like Beethoven show the world how much could be accomplished even with such a "handicap?" So you see it is not always to be considered a handicap.

Earaches

What causes earaches?

Earaches are a reflection of anger about what you are hearing. They are more prevalent in children because most children either can't or won't acknowledge the anger that they feel about what they hear.

<u>Headaches</u>

Let us end this chapter with the inclusion of headaches. Some head-aches are a result of brain injuries. When a person has an "accident" which results in a brain injury or when a person develops a brain tumor, it is a big cry for attention. You have permitted yourself to feel so diminished or invisible that you are crying out to be noticed. It is a plea that says, "Help me. Pay attention to me. I feel over-whelmed. I feel very scared. I need someone to care about me." An injury of this magnitude would require special care and treatment. It affords you the opportunity to examine your position with regards to others and your life circumstances. It encourages you to set your priorities. It forces you to deal with fears. It shows you that there are changes that you need to make in order to feel better about yourself and to function differently. It shows you your strengths and your weaknesses. It is a marvelous opportunity for personal growth.

Some headaches are classified as migraine. They are headaches that are so painful that they become incapacitating. The reasons behind migraines are the same reasons behind the other aches in the head area but to a deeper degree. You have let your fears go so deep that you are sabotaging yourself by becoming non-functioning in order to escape them. In other words, your fears have become so scary to you that you even have a fear of dealing with them. Headaches are also a way of punishing yourself for things that you have imagined that you have done wrong. You don't have to be perfect. Again, that's my job. Trying to be perfect just makes for added stress. You are "good enough, smart enough, creative enough, beautiful enough, and worthy enough." Stop being angry with yourself. Forgive yourself. Find your self-worth and accept it. Be the beautiful spirit that you already are—just as you are.

Epilogue

I would like to leave you with some final thoughts. Each of you has the capability to attain all of your heart's desires. How can this be accomplished if you haven't considered what it is that you really wish? You notice that I did not use the term "want." It is for you to decide if you wish to be "wanting" in your life. In which areas of your life do you presently "want?" Are you content with how things are now? Are there any areas of your life that you wish to change? If you desire to see a metamorphosis, either in your physical, emotional, or mental world, then you must do the work required.

1. Begin by noticing where your discontentment lies. Look at the things that you have created in each area of your life. Look at the people that you have drawn into your life.

2. Decide if you are really ready to release the reasons that you have created and retained your situation. If you are still receiving a payback for whatever reason and are not ready to release your condition that's okay. No one is judging you. No one is criticizing you. There is no time limit on how long you stay where you are. There is no time limit on how long you keep your ailments. It is your choice of preference.

3. If you are ready to make changes fully examine the underlying cause or causes of your conditions or predicaments. Everything has been brought into your life for a good reason. It is up to you to figure out why you are where you are. Look for the blessing in every situation.

4. Roll up your sleeves and do what you need to do to make the necessary changes. This book is full of questions to help you to make decisions. Make a workbook for yourself. Start a journal. Do the meditations in this book.

5. When you have done the work required for change, maintain a positive attitude. Believe in your abilities. Know that even if change is not immediately noticeable it really is taking place.

6. Continue to reinforce your belief with frequent positive affirmations. Keep talking to yourself and visualizing yourself in your newly developed form.

7. Give yourself all the time you need. You are eternal.

8. Love yourself. Be gentle with yourself. Treat yourself with respect. You are a special being. You are a part of God.

9. Forgive yourself. You are worth it.

10. Don't quit.

I leave you with these words: My children, you can do it! You can create your lives any way that you wish. You can heal anything that you have created. Believe. Know that anything is possible. Have faith.

Reading Suggestions

Andrews, Ted. *How to See and Read the Aura.* Minnesota: Llewellyn Publications, 1952.

Borysenko, Joan, and Borysenko, Miroslav. *The Power of the Mind to Heal.* California: Hay House, Inc.,1994.

Bowers, Barbara. *What Color is Your Aura?* New York: Pocket Books, 1989.

Brennan, Barbara Ann. *Hands of Light: A Guide to Healing Through the Human Energy Field.* New York: Bantam, 1987.

————. *Light Emerging: The Journal of Personal Healing.* New York: Bantam, 1993.

Buscaglia, Leo. *Loving Each Other.* New Jersey: Slack Incorporated, 1984.

Chopra, Deepak. *Creating Health.* Boston: Houghton Mifflin Company, 1991.

Dyer, Dr. Wayne W. *You'll See It When You Believe It.* New York: Avon Books, 1989.

Hay, Louise L. *You Can Heal Your Life.* California: Hay House, Inc., 1984.

Myss, Caroline. *Anatomy of the Spirit.* New York: Three Rivers Press, 1996.

————. *Why People Don't Heal and How They Can.* New York: Three Rivers Press, 1997.

Siegel, Bernie S. *Peace, Love, & Healing.* New York: Harper Collins Publishers, Inc, 1989.

Walsch, Neale Donald. *Conversations with God an uncommon dialogue, book 1.* Virginia: Hampton Roads Publishing Company, Inc, 1995.

————. *Conversations with God .an uncommon dialogue. book 2.* Virginia: Hampton Roads Publishing Company, Inc, 1997.

————. *Conversations with God, .an uncommon dialogue. book 3.* Virginia: Hampton Roads Publishing, Inc., 1998.

Weil, Andrew. *Natural Health, Natural Medicine.* Boston: Houghton Mifflin Company, 1998.

Index

0-595-31493-7

Printed in the United States
20149LVS00003B/136-195

9 780595 314935